THE LIFE

MONACO GRAND PRIX

THE
LIFE

MONACO GRAND PRIX

motorbooks

STUART CODLING

© 2019 Quarto Publishing Group USA Inc.
Text © 2019 Stuart Codling

First published in 2019 by Motorbooks, an imprint of The Quarto Group, 100 Cummings Center Suite 265D, Beverly, MA 01915 USA. T (978) 282-9590 F (978) 283-2742 www.QuartoKnows.com

10 9 8 7 6 5 4 3 2 1

ISBN: 978-0-7603-6374-4

Library of Congress Cataloging-in-Publication Data

Names: Codling, Stuart, 1972- author.
Title: The Life Monaco Grand Prix / Stuart Codling.
Other titles: Monaco Grand Prix
Description: Minneapolis, Minnesotas : Motorbooks, an imprint of
The Quarto Group, 2019. | "Digital edition published in 2018"—
T.p. verso.
Identifiers: LCCN 2018033825| ISBN 9780760363744 (hardcover) |
ISBN 9780760363751 (Digital edition)
Subjects: LCSH: Grand Prix de Monaco (Automobile race)—History.
| Monaco--History. | Monaco--Description and travel. | Automobile
racing drivers—Biography. | Riviera (France)—Description and travel.
Classification: LCC GV1034.68.M63 C63 2019 | DDC
796.7209449/49—dc23
LC record available at https://lccn.loc.gov/2018033825

Acquiring Editor: Zack Miller
Project Manager: Alyssa Bluhm
Series Creative Director: Laura Drew
Page Design and Layout: Laura Drew and Beth Middleworth

Printed in China

MIX
Paper from
responsible sources
FSC® C016973

MON

CONTENTS

PREFACE

MONACO

WHY MONACO

A tumbling tangle of streets clutching at a rockface-like vegetation. Sapphire-blue Mediterranean waves crashing against Le Rocher, the impassive rocky promontory that rears up in defiance of both the elements and ancient land-based foes. A city-state almost hewn from the stone itself.

Monaco is many things. Industrious and yet industry-less (unless you count tourism, gambling, and fish farming). Fiercely independent of spirit and yet beholden to neighboring France for defense. Above all, it is tiny: the land border is just 3.7 miles long.

And yet, this microstate possesses a powerful mystique and occupies a special place in pop culture, founded upon roots that feel as old as the rocks upon which it perches. Small the Principality of Monaco may be, but neighboring states larger and more powerful have come and gone and passed into the domain of history. Medieval and Renaissance-era wars have crashed upon the rocks and receded, the petty ambitions of wannabe emperors and kings from near and far thwarted, leaving Monaco largely as it was. Its rulers have played the game of thrones and survived.

Later threads in this historic tapestry command greater attention now. Around two-thirds of Monaco residents are foreigners, drawn by the razzle-dazzle of Hollywood glamour, annual motor racing events such as the Monte Carlo Rally and the Formula 1 Grand Prix, the Monte-Carlo Masters tennis tournament, the casino, and the absence of income tax levied on non-French residents.

The Formula 1 race is the principal historic connection between Monaco as it was and Monaco as it is. First held in 1929, when the Principality's wealth and status hinged upon receipts from its casinos, the grand prix has continued to fly the flag for a certain kind of glamour in a more hard-headed postwar era. World War II scattered most casino punters to the four winds, and in the decades since, Monaco's economy has become dependent on overseas residents sheltering their liquidity under the rock, no questions asked.

Literary greats including F. Scott Fitzgerald, Graham Greene, and W. Somerset Maugham (whose pithy description of Monaco as "a sunny place for shady people" has become increasingly ubiquitous and, in recent years, accurate) exquisitely captured

and immortalized the light and shade
of the French Riviera, with Monaco at
its heart. Less self-consciously rarefied
art forms trod diligently in their foot-
steps: in the insouciant caper movie
To Catch A Thief, celebrated director
Alfred Hitchcock weaves a tale of a
retired Cote d'Azur cat burglar, played
by the suitably debonair Cary Grant,
having to prove himself innocent of a
series of high-profile heists by snaring
the real thief. Naturally, he meets and
falls in love with a beautiful heiress,
played by Grace Kelly, whose life tra-
jectory would carry her into the orbit
of Monaco royalty and, sadly, a tragic
demise on the mountain. Kelly married
Prince Rainier III, Europe's most eligible bachelor, who had assumed the
throne after his mother renounced it—
having become romantically entangled
with a notorious criminal nicknamed
Rene la Canne (literally, "Rene the
walking stick").

Fiction, you see, has nothing on real
life in Monaco, then and now . . .

CHAPTER ONE

THE MAKING OF MONACO

DYNASTY WARS

The Rock of Monaco's strategic and easily defensible position on the French coast made it a small but pivotal element in the ongoing dynastic power politics that ravaged this area of Europe in the pre-Renaissance era. Though archaeological evidence exists of human occupation dating back to 400,000 BC, little exists in the way of definitive written records. It's likely that the name Monaco derives from a tribe known as the Monoïkos, colonists of Greek descent, who occupied the area in the sixth century BC.

Occupation is a tenuous concept at best, because for many years this area notionally belonged to the Romans, who erected the Tropaeum Alpium—also known as the Trophy of Augustus—in nearby La Turbie during the summer of 6 BC. This monument to Octavius, Julius Caesar's nephew and the future Emperor Augustus, today stands partially intact at what was the border between Rome and Gaul (ancient France). Restored in the 1930s, the monument is believed to have stood at nearly 50 meters (164 feet) high when first built; a stone, transcribed by Pliny the Elder, lists the forty-four Ligurian tribes that Octavius forcefully prevailed upon to cease and desist from interrupting lucrative trade routes through the region. Even then, it seems, this area of the coastline had a reputation for banditry.

Following the collapse of the Western Roman Empire, this region lapsed into chaotic squabbling. What is now known as Italy was a loose and frangible network of constantly maneuvering city-states and republics—one of which, Genoa, absorbed Monaco and its surrounding areas as it expanded aggressively between the tenth and fourteenth centuries. Trade and sea power extended Genovese influence eastwards as far as northern Egypt and what we now know as Israel and Lebanon, as well as into the Black Sea and onwards to Crimea; westwards along the French coast into the Iberian peninsula; and southwards to Carthage and other pockets of the north African coastline.

Though the Holy Roman Emperor (a title invented by Charlemagne three centuries after the fall of the empire itself, and the subject of considerable ongoing political dispute and outright warfare) notionally ruled over Genoa, with the city's Bishop acting as president, in practice the real power resided with elected consuls—a

François GRIMALDI

"MALIZIA"

1297 - 1997

system imitating the glory days of Rome. And, just as it had in Rome, this system enabled wealthy trading families to access, wield, and extend power for themselves. Fault lines naturally developed between these families, including the Adorno, the Fieschi, the Spinola, the Doria, and the Grimaldi, as they sought to maximize their own wealth and influence at the expense of the others.

Over the course of centuries, control of Genoa swung between these plotting dynasties, and occasionally tensions between them and their wider allies would reach the point where swords were drawn. Thus, it was that in 1271 the Grimaldis and their allies were expelled from Genoa, and although five years later the Pope brokered a peace enabling them to return, not all of them did, and the factional rancor continued.

The fragmented nature of historical records at this time means the actual evidence for Monaco's official origin story is patchy. Nevertheless, officially, modern Monaco's history begins on the night of January 8, 1297, when Franceso Grimaldi and his cousin Rainier launched a sneak attack on Spinoza-held Monaco. Gaining free admittance to the castle while disguised as a Franciscan monk, Grimaldi drew his sword once inside, threw the door open for his men, and overpowered the garrison.

The moment is enshrined in the Monegasque coat of arms, which features two monks bearing swords.

Swashbuckling, sneaky, and with a flair for the dramatic—whether Monaco's preferred narrative of its origin is true or not is almost beside the point. Barring a few interruptions, for over seven centuries Grimaldi and his anointed successors (not all biological) have clung to the rock. After the family were forced to flee in 1301 by Genovese forces, Rainier's son Charles spent thirty years plotting to acquire Monaco once more; having done so, he took advantage of territorial disputes between Genoa and the Crown of Aragon (now part of Spain) to extend Grimaldi rule to neighboring Menton and Roquebrun.

Monaco's growing power—not to mention a growing reputation as a haven for pirates—drove the Genovese to invade it again in 1357. Charles and his son Rainier II were driven out and never returned.

Yet, still the Grimaldis coveted their rock, growing their wealth through trade until Rainier's sons Antoine, Ambrose, and Jean bought Monaco, by then owned by the Crown of Aragon, in 1419. It was Jean who enshrined in the Principality's constitution that the royal title's succession would pass to the reigning prince's first-born male child—an article that would require considerable fudging through the years as various princes failed to deliver legitimate male heirs.

Small and economically fragile, yet strategically important to trade, Monaco was defensible thanks to the castle on the rock, but not invulnerable. Neighboring powers coveted it as they consolidated their own territory and warred with each other; Genoa faded, but Gaul completed its transformation into what we now know as France under a succession of ambitious monarchs. Likewise, the Christian reconquest of the Iberian Peninsula, followed by some strategic dynastic unions, led to states such as the Crown of Aragon coalescing into what we now know as Spain, ambitious to conquer worlds both old and new. To survive, the Grimaldis had to hustle, strategically divesting themselves of Menton and Roquebrun to forge allegiances with their neighbors. Until the seventeenth century, Grimaldi rulers would not dare adopt royal nomenclature, styling themselves as lords rather than princes.

In 1489, the King of France officially recognized Monaco's independence, but this was just a small victory in the state's ongoing struggle to assert its identity. Perhaps it was for the best that its rulers had acquired a reputation for hot blood, combative temperament, and always carrying a sword in hand.

CHAPTER TWO

THE PRINCE SANCTIONS A RACE

INDEPENDENCE AND REBELLION

Popular folklore has it that when Honoré II died in 1662, forcing his grandson Louis I and free-spirited wife Catherine Charlotte de Gramont to depart the French king's court and return to Monaco, Catherine Charlotte cried throughout the journey while one of her lovers shadowed the couple south wearing heavy disguise. For all the rich artworks within the castle, it still had the austere external aspect of a fortress, presiding over a plain-looking harbor village that numbered but a handful of streets.

Over the following two hundred years, Monaco changed almost beyond recognition. By the end of the nineteenth century, propelled headlong by the advance of technology and the arrival of mass transport such as the railway, the newly independent principality existed in a state of perpetual redevelopment. It was an unashamedly wealth-driven transition from sleepy harbor town surrounded by groves of lemon and olive trees, the hillside studded with villas occupied by European gentry enjoying privacy and the winter climate, to an altogether more hard-edged domain. Ordinary Monégasques began to grow disenchanted as their home changed

around them, a disposition that hardened into rancor with the growing perception that foreigners were enjoying a disproportionate share of the proceeds.

Monaco's tendency towards mild winter weather had always encouraged the privileged to shelter from less favorable climates; now tax breaks enabled them to shelter their wealth from scrutiny. This corner of the Riviera became rather less genteel, but while this discouraged some visitors, there were plenty of others cut from less discriminating cloth,

> "THE PRINCE RETURNED TO MONACO AND WAS SHOCKED TO FIND HIS SUBJECTS GREETED HIM NOT WITH THE CUSTOMARY FANFARE BUT WITH HISSES AND JEERS."
> —MARK BRAUDE, *MAKING MONTE CARLO*

OTÉRO

ReutLinger
PARIS

eager to try their luck at the tables and sample the stock of the wine cellar at the Hôtel de Paris, famed for having a kilometer of rack space occupied by rarefied vintages.

Prince Albert I already had one annulled marriage behind him when he ascended to the throne in 1889, age forty. His first wife, a product of the Scottish gentry, had fled back to her homeland while Albert was fighting in the Franco-Prussian War, and the annulment required papal dispensation for their son Louis to retain his legitimacy. This, and the not entirely happy marriage that followed—Albert married the Dowager Duchess de Richelieu in 1889, but they separated in 1902, providing no male issue—has subsequently provided further fuel for those who choose to believe in the curse of the Grimaldis. So too did the memoirs of the Spanish dancer and courtesan Carolina "La Belle" Otero, who claimed to have enjoyed close enough relations with Albert to record that he suffered from erectile dysfunction.

Of perhaps more import to the well-being of the principality was Albert's growing distance from the people he ruled absolutely. In the years immediately before and after the dissolution of his second marriage, Albert immersed himself in the relatively new science of oceanography, undertaking expeditions to locations as distant and varied as the Azores and the Arctic Ocean (in which an archipelago is now named after him).

Meanwhile, the gulf between citizens and visitors widened and deepened. The mathematics were indisputable: Monégasques were barred from gambling in the casinos or working for the monopoly company that owned them, and there was very little industry or agriculture elsewhere in the domain, so while they paid no tax they also earned very little. And while existing in this state of penury, they shared the same tiny patch of seaside real estate with foreign citizens—predominantly French—who took the best jobs and flaunted the rewards. And, year on year, the wealth the Monégasques did not share resulted in rising prices that exacerbated their state of poverty.

Petitions circulated, to little effect. In March 1910, a man called Suffren Reymond set in motion what is now known as *Le Réveil Monégasque* (The Monégasque Awakening), sufficiently revving up a huge crowd at a public meeting for eight hundred of them to accompany him to the palace and hand an ultimatum to the prince himself. With unctuous words, Albert and his chief of staff accepted the ultimatum,

but then did little enough to put it into practice that the citizens of Monaco continued to protest noisily and with increasing frequency. Within weeks, Albert was appealing to France to keep troops on hand in case the lingering specter of armed revolt became a reality. Guns were stockpiled in the wine cellar of the Hôtel de Paris to guard against the prospect.

Events in Monaco were significant enough to warrant being mentioned in dispatches as far afield as the US. An editorial in the *New York Times* on December 11, 1910, headlined "Is Monaco Doomed? Other Nations Want It," outlined the scenario: "At first sight one would imagine the Monégasques had every reason to be satisfied, since, thanks to the money paid by the gambling syndicate into the princely exchequer, the people are exempt from all taxation. But although they may not actually pay rates and taxes, they earn next to nothing. The principality has no industrial or agricultural resources. It lives on its visitors. But the very people who thrive and fatten upon the visitors are themselves strangers, namely, Frenchmen, who are favored every way by the reigning Prince, and by the gambling syndicate, all the employees of the latter being French. The natives do not share in the spoils and are in the

PRINCE OF MONACO   5456-2

PRINCE OF MONACO + COL. CODY.

> **"PRINCE ALBERT HONORÉ CHARLES, UNTIL NOW ABSOLUTE IN THE GOVERNMENT OF MONACO, DECREED TODAY THE ELECTION OF A PARLIAMENT THROUGH UNIVERSAL SUFFRAGE."**
>
> — *NEW YORK TIMES,* MARCH 29, 1910

position of a starving man, tantalized by the tempting sight of a well-spread table to which he is not invited . . . If the Monégasques have their way, they will put an end to the agreement existing between this malodorous gambling hell concern and Prince Albert on the ground that the contract is invalidated by immorality, according to the jurisprudence of every civilized country, and also because, they argue, that no sovereign, be he absolute monarch or constitutional ruler, has the right to turn over control of his dominions to a public gambling hell concern against the

wishes of his people, or to sacrifice the good name of the latter and to cover it with world-wide infamy for the sake of his own selfish personal gain."

The piece painted Monaco as a thoroughly dissolute and degenerate destination in comparison with "respectable" neighbors such as Nice, and reserved its most sneering tone for a brief history of the Grimaldi family line, alighting upon Prince Florestan (Albert's grandfather), who had been a theatre actor during Napoleon's reign and married the daughter of a Parisian butcher. "This actor Prince and his plebian wife are about the only occupants of the throne of Monaco who seem to have ever lived happily together. The matrimonial experiences of all the others have been most unfortunate."

And, as the *New York Times* editorial alluded, neighboring powers—France, Italy, and Germany—coveted Monaco's wealth and strategic location and were eying each other suspiciously. Europe would not go to war until 1914, but all the preconditions existed for it. Prince Albert gave ground, granting concessions such as freedom of the press, but he was unwilling to give up his rich source of income to a braying mob who seemed determined to re-enact the temple and evicting the money-changers. Neither could he easily satisfy their desire for autonomy, since Monaco was committed to remain a monarchy under a secret provision within the terms of the 1861 treaty with France that had granted it independence.

When protesters stormed the palace in October that year, forcing Albert to flee over the border to France for safety, it crystallized the issue. Fearful that Germany was machinating to foment rebellion and install his cousin as prince, with a view to establishing Monaco as a German naval base, Albert drew up a constitution in which he retained his executive powers while a hierarchy of advisory councils composed of elected Monégasques (including Suffren Reymond) took care of day-to-day government. It was ratified on January 5, 1911.

The days of Monaco as an absolute monarchy were over—in theory.

A THOROUGHLY IMPRACTICAL EVENT

Contemporary readers will probably take ownership of a motorcar for granted. In the late nineteenth century, it was anything but everyday transport.

It epitomized a certain kind of pushiness and ostentation that did not sit well with ordinary folk across Europe—in many countries there were those who saw the "auto-car" as a fiendish and terrifying invention and an unwelcome presence on the roads. Many pressure groups argued that car owners should be preceded on the highway by a person carrying a red flag, so that livestock and persons of a nervous disposition could be alerted to its approach.

So, to many, the car's challenge to the preeminence of the horse and cart was a nonstarter. But not to the moneyed set in Monaco, who were early adopters of this novel form of transport. In 1890, just four years after Karl Benz publicly unveiled his Patent-Motorwagen, Alexandre Noghès—a descendent of the commander of the Spanish garrison installed by the regent in 1605—founded the Sport Vélocipédique Monégasque, a sporting club for owners of cars and bicycles.

The principality itself, though roughly half the size of New York's Central Park and blessed with few truly flat roads, became a showcase for high-class automobiles (adding somewhat to the angst of the relatively impoverished ordinary Monégasques). For the kind of person who liked to travel individually, rather than swaying several people deep on the train, the horse-and-carriage was *so* last century. Rolls-Royces, Daimlers, Argylls, Packards, Loziers, De Dion-Boutons, and their ilk displaced equine transport from the prime spots outside the casino and hotels.

While Monaco attracted a relatively continuous flow of gambling traffic, tourism was largely seasonal, apart from the established regulars from around Europe who liked to "winter" in the principality's relatively mild climate. Noghès and his club's grandees hit upon the notion of showcasing this virtue with an event that would draw like-minded car enthusiasts from across Europe during the winter months. The Monte Carlo Rally was born.

By practical necessity, the Rally, first held in 1911, hot on the heels of

the promulgation of Monaco's constitution, was more of a test than a race. Other circular or point-to-point road races such as the Targa Florio were already established in the calendar. The roads both within Monaco itself and connecting to it from without were considered unsuitable for such an event. So, the first Monte Carlo Rally would be a contest of elegance and quality over speed, with no set route.

There were twenty-three entries, of which twenty started, hailing from as far afield as Paris, Berlin, Vienna, and Geneva. Participants had to drive their road car from their place of origin to Monaco carrying a prominent identification plate announcing their participation in the "Rallye Automobile Monaco." It was influencer marketing long before that term was coined.

On arrival, and having no doubt enjoyed the transition from foul weather to beatific winter sun as the Monégasque vista opened up before them, they received a score according to a points system that encompassed distance traveled, the elegance of the car, its state upon arrival, and the state of the passengers and their luggage. As you might expect, this subjectivity led to the results being hotly disputed. Henri Rougier, an automobile dealer and racer, was judged the winner.

> **"THERE WERE GRANDS PRIX ALL OVER EUROPE AND NOGHES SAW NO REASON WHY HIS 'COUNTRY' SHOULDN'T HAVE ONE TOO."**
> **—RENE DREYFUS,** *MY TWO LIVES*

Entries swelled in subsequent years as the event grew in popularity. In March 1925, the Sport Vélocipédique Monégasque voted to change its name to the Automobile Club de Monaco (ACM), with a sporting committee overseen by Noghès's son Antony, who had played a prominent role in the first rally's organization and its evolution into a preeminent annual event.

Antony Noghès had even greater ambitions to establish Monaco as a fixture on the international sporting calendar. First, though, he would need a mandate. To be a national car club in more than just name, the ACM had to be recognized by the Paris-based Association Internationale des Automobile-Clubs Reconnus (International Association of Recognized Automobile Clubs), the ancestor of what we now know as the Fédération Internationale de l'Automobile (FIA), the governing organization of world motorsports. This august body sent Noghès on his way with a resounding *non*, on the grounds that Monaco's rally didn't take place on its sovereign territory, so the ACM didn't merit the status of a national sporting authority.

This presented a hurdle Noghès could only vault by committing to running an international motor-racing event on the narrow, twisting, rutted streets of Monaco itself. A lesser individual might have balked at the task, but Noghès was nothing if not ambitious. And he would have a high-profile ally in making it happen: none other than Prince Louis II himself.

Louis had a vested interest in polishing Monaco's status. The product of Albert I's annulled first marriage, he had been legitimized by the Pope as a constitutional fudge since Albert sired no further male heirs. He was not particularly close to his father, having left his mother. While the principality had remained neutral in World War I under the rule of his father, Louis served in the French army.

He had already fathered an illegitimate daughter with a cabaret singer, and with no further offspring in the offing—he was forty-seven at the end of the war, and unmarried—a further piece of legislatory legerdemain had to be enacted. In 1918, Prince Albert passed a law enshrining the principle that the succession could pass to an adopted heir, and a year later Louis formally adopted his illegitimate daughter, Charlotte, decisively heading off the claim of the German cousin Wilhelm of Urach. Louis ascended in June 1922 upon the death of Prince Albert, aged fifty-one.

Though Louis later acquired a reputation for benign neglect, as honorary president of the ACM he signed off on Noghès's risky endeavor. So too did the all-powerful hotel and casino operating company, whose funds would be necessary to promote the putative Monaco-based road race.

With political will and sufficient capital behind him, Noghès was on his way. But there remained the greatest obstacle of all: the inscrutable topography of Monaco itself.

PRINCESS OF MONACO

WALKING THE ROUTE

Hosting a motor-racing event on closed public roads was not at all without precedent, for that was how the sport had come into being. Even by the 1920s, as cars became more affordable and ownership more socially acceptable, even desirable, racing was predominantly the domain of wealthy individuals. Purpose-built circuits did exist, following the lead of the groundbreaking Brooklands in the UK and the Indianapolis Motor Speedway in the US, but these kinds of facilities required huge investment and political will, not to mention available real estate.

The question of who should govern motor racing had been solved to some extent when a number of prominent national motoring clubs formed their own trade body, the Association Internationale des Automobile-Clubs Reconnus, in 1904. Categorizing events and codifying rules was a far greater challenge, given the limits of long-distance communication and the huge spread of machinery. Gradually, almost by trial and error, accepted formats came into being: the practice of having a "riding mechanic" in each car was dispensed with; and at an increasing number of events, mass starts replaced the established process of setting entrants off at timed intervals. Car manufacturers came and went in a factory-supported capacity as quarrels developed over what kind of cars could compete: Should there be a "formula," grading cars by size, weight, and engine displacement, or should it be a free-for-all (also known as "Formula Libre")? The result was that events calling themselves "grands prix" sprung up all over the place, offering a variety of formats and incentives, enabling competitors to pick and choose. A common denominator

> "THE COURSE WAS EXTREMELY TRICKY AND INCLUDED INNUMERABLE BENDS AND TWO HAIRPINS. IT HAD TO BE COVERED ONE HUNDRED TIMES."
>
> —*MOTOR SPORT* MAGAZINE, MAY 1929

was the practice of businesses and local stakeholders banding together to offer prizes to lure the best competitors, knowing that this would draw crowds to their town.

These facts will have played upon Noghès's mind as he wandered the streets of Monaco, trying to alight upon a suitable event format and route. What had once been three distinct settlements—the fortress-cum-palace on the Rock, the village now known as Monte Carlo on the promontory opposite, and the fishing-village-cum-trading-port of La Condamine in between—had grown together, but the streets were mostly a tangle of cobbled alleyways, and on such boulevards as were wide enough to justify the name, cars shared the road with trams. As a businessman as well as an enthusiast—his family was in the tobacco trade—Noghès recognized the tourism value of setting the route through the heart of Monaco itself, passing iconic locations such as the grand casino.

Ultimately, the route, rushing along a cliff face and passing through a tunnel, suggested itself: "This skirted the port," Noghès would say later, "passing along the quay and the Boulevard Albert Premier, climbed the hill of Monte Carlo, then passed round the Place du Casino, took the downhill zigzag near Monte Carlo Station to get back approximately to sea level and from there, along the Boulevard Louis II and the Tir aux Pigeons tunnel, the course came back to the port quayside.

"Today," he concluded, "the roads comprising this circuit look as though they were made for the purpose."

At the time, laced with cobblestones and tram rails, many of them were not. Noghès chipped away at any lingering opposition, helped by high-profile support from Louis Chiron, the one-time nightclub dancer who had risen to prominence as a successful racer of Bugatti and Alfa Romeo grand prix machinery.

In October 1928, the ACM was officially admitted to the Association Internationale des Automobile-Clubs Reconnus (AIACR), and a date was set for the very first Monaco Grand Prix: April 14, 1929. In the intervening months, Noghès raced against the clock to make the roads ready and invite a sufficiently glittering international cast of stars.

The winner of that historic first race, though, was a complete surprise.

CHAPTER THREE

DANCER, RACER, SOLDIER, SPY

LOUIS CHIRON, GIGOLO AND RACER

Still arguably the most famous and successful racing driver to have been born in Monaco, as opposed to adopting it as a place of residence, the vivacious, debonair, and ambitious Louis Chiron also hailed from less privileged stock than many of his contemporaries on the international scene. In an era when most racing drivers were scions of the aristocracy or commerce-related "new money," Chiron parlayed his many talents to pull himself up by the bootstraps.

That's not to say he was a child of the streets. Chiron's parents were French, a nationality that enjoyed greater work privileges than native Monégasques at the time of Chiron's birth in 1899. Chiron's father was the maître d' at the Hôtel de Paris, and Chiron grew up in this milieu, working as a bellboy and groom and acquiring the necessary personal skills in dealing with high society confidently while maintaining due deference.

When war came, Chiron signed up as an artilleryman in the French army. It's been subsequently claimed that he became the personal driver for Marshal Ferdinand Foch, commander in chief on the western front and later the supreme allied commander. Whatever the truth of this, he returned from the theatre of conflict a highly competent driver at the age of nineteen. Back in Monaco, he found employment as a professional dance partner at the Hôtel de Paris, where he proved himself as sure-footed on the dance floor—and with a succession of wealthy women—as he was behind the wheel of a car.

Through the patronage of at least one of his dancing partners, Chiron acquired a Bugatti Type 13 Brescia, a development of a prewar design that was proving surprisingly competitive in postwar racing, thanks to its light weight and punchy multivalve 1.4-liter engine. Bugatti had added the "Brescia" tag after scoring a 1-2-3-4 finish in the 1921 Brescia Grand Prix. Chiron's performances in his little "voiturette" earned him enough prize money to step up a class and buy a Type 35 Grand Prix car—and eventually earn a call-up to Bugatti's works team.

Chiron's activities in racing circles also brought him into contact with Alfred Hoffman, youngest son of the founder of the Hoffman-La Roche pharmaceutical company and a wannabe industrialist through his own Nerka spark plug company. Hoffman, a racing enthusiast, became Chiron's patron, though

the two would ultimately become estranged after Chiron had an affair with his wife. Born in America to a Swedish-German father and Norwegian mother, Alice Hoffman-Trobeck—nicknamed "Baby"—was multilingual and urbane, a born traveler, and as passionate about motor racing as her husband.

Backed by both Bugatti and Hoffman, Chiron achieved outstanding results in competition. Over the course of 1928, he won seven grands prix in Europe, including the Italian Grand Prix on the combined oval and road course at Monza, where he beat Varzi and Nuvolari.

Chiron was the toast of Monaco, and it was his explicit support of Antony Noghès's outré project that gave the concept of the Monaco Grand Prix a final nudge over the finishing line. To his eternal regret, though, Chiron was unable to take part in the inaugural event of 1929—Hoffman had arranged for him to contest the Indy 500. The *Indianapolis News* hailed the arrival of the "European champion" in his "record-breaking car," naming him "the most dangerous contender Europe has sent to American speedways in many years." Chiron's presence was clearly newsworthy, though his performance wasn't up to that of the frontrunners, and Chiron

qualified mid-grid and raced to seventh place behind eventual winner Ray Keech.

But Chiron's connections in the racing world—and a prize pot of 100,000 francs—ensured a healthy response to the invitations for the first Monaco Grand Prix. Caracciola was perhaps the biggest star present, along with Philippe Étancelin, Baron Philippe de Rothschild (racing under an assumed name), and René Dreyfus.

By now Chiron's dalliance with "Baby" was in the public domain, but it would be another two years before Hoffman fired him. Bugatti also let him go, not for want of wins—but because he was not what they viewed as a team player. Chiron threw his lot in with Caracciola as an independent, planning to run their own team, Scuderia CC, with Alfa Romeo P3 machinery, but Caracciola broke his leg in an enormous crash at Tabac on the team's debut in the 1933 Monaco Grand Prix. That put Scuderia CC on ice, but Chiron found a berth with Alfa Romeo's works team, run by Enzo Ferrari.

Now thirty-four, Chiron was old enough for rivals to label him "the wily old fox." William Boddy, in Chiron's obituary for the eminent

Motor Sport magazine in 1979, wrote: "His abilities were unabated, his turn out still immaculate, his wild gestures to his pit enjoyed by those who knew the game."

Perhaps his finest hour behind the wheel came in the 1934 French Grand Prix at Montlhéry in the face of new opposition from the German teams Mercedes and Auto Union, making their international debut. The silver cars, blessed by the Nazi regime as a prestige project, had the best drivers money could buy and all the engineering resources they required. They were on a mission to win.

Memories of the last war were fresh enough for this to be a distasteful prospect for the French fans, not least since their neighbor was now led by a brutal, aggressive, and openly warlike regime. In hellishly hot and dusty conditions, the German cars took off seemingly into the distance. Chiron played his Alfa with the smoothness and delicacy of a concert pianist, and his exquisitely paced victory as the silver cars gradually fell by the wayside gave cause for great cheer, inking his status as a national hero.

This charming if occasionally difficult character was destined not to add to his tally of Monaco Grand Prix

wins, but when he returned to the competitive fray after World War II, he established a record that stands to this day: in 1955 he qualified nineteenth and finished sixth in a one-off outing at Monaco in a Lancia D50, at the age of fifty-five, making him the oldest driver to contest a world championship grand prix.

For over two decades after his retirement, Chiron held the post of president of the Automobile Club de Monaco and commissaire général of the principality's two major international races. It was he who waved the starting flag at the Monaco Grand Prix well into his dotage, no longer one of the key protagonists but most definitely among the undisputed stars of the show.

"AT MONACO CHIRON, ALWAYS DEBONAIR, SUNBURNED ROUND FACE UNDER CLOTH HELMET, DROVE AS IMPECCABLY AS EVER."

—WILLIAM BODDY

WHATEVER HAPPENED TO
THE FIRST GP WINNER?

Shortly after 5:00 a.m. on Saturday, April 13, 1929, the beleaguered residents of Monaco were awoken by the roar of a 2.3-liter straight-eight Bugatti engine as a lone T35B circulated the temporary racecourse on the principality's streets. They had endured the sound of racing engines running between 5:30 a.m. and 7:00 a.m. on previous days but had been assured this would not be the case on Saturday. Nevertheless, that sound . . .

The man behind the wheel had only just arrived for the Grand Prix and was making up for lost practice time. Some say he had been intending to race in Italy but had changed plans at the last minute. Whatever, he was a friend of Louis Chiron, and an established winner at grand prix level, so his wish was granted. Very few people, though, could tell you who this mysterious "W Williams" was.

How William Grover-Williams lived and died remains shrouded in mystery. Accounts differ: We can be reasonably certain that he was born in France in 1903, the son of a horse breeder who had moved to Paris along with his principal client, a Russian nobleman, and that at

some point in his life, his father also worked as a chauffeur. Until recently, it was reasonably well established that Grover-Williams was recruited by the Special Operations Executive in World War II, that he worked as a spy for the allies, and that he was betrayed and captured and eventually shot in Sachsenhausen concentration camp in spring 1945. But in the years that followed, rumors persisted on the racing scene that he had survived the camp and that he had worked for a time with MI6, the British intelligence service, who had faked such paperwork as existed documenting his execution. After that, narratives diverged. Some stories had him running a grocery in Godalming, England; others claimed he moved back in with his wife and lived in France under a false identity, only meeting his demise when he was knocked off his bicycle by a car in 1983.

In 1929, Grover-Williams was a successful racing driver, albeit one competing under a pseudonym so as to disguise his activities from his family. How he came by the capital to acquire his first racing cars is a topic of some speculation, but he was gifted and successful enough

to be occasionally employed by the Bugatti factory team, which is where he encountered Chiron, who later invited him to compete in the inaugural Monaco Grand Prix.

Grover-Williams was soon to be married, having met and fallen in love with the mistress of the successful Irish portrait artist William Orpen, Yvonne Aubicq. His reasoning was that being seen to be painting a civilian subject would have got him into trouble with his employers; as it happened, spies were a sensitive subject, and he was recalled to London and narrowly escaped a court martial. After the war, he maintained studios in London and Paris, and kept his relationship with Aubicq ticking over while still married to his wife of twenty years. Cleaving to stereotype, Orpen was a heavy drinker, but his success enabled him to retain a suite at the Hotel Astoria in Paris, a separate house for Aubicq, and a retinue that included a chauffeur for the Rolls-Royce he acquired in 1923: William Grover-Williams.

The chauffeur bought a second-hand Hispano-Suiza and became a racing driver in 1926, following this up with the acquisition of a Bugatti, source of capital unknown. Until this point, his racing activities had been confined to motorcycles, where he first used the pseudonym "W Williams,"

but from the early months of 1926, he established himself as a competitive force on four wheels.

This was a good time to be an independent racer, because motorsport's Paris-based governing body had tied its proverbial shoelaces together in trying to lay down a technical formula that would appeal to race promoters and manufacturers alike. Over the remainder of the decade, continuous tinkering with the rules governing car weight and engine displacement had the unfortunate consequence of chasing out manufacturers such as Alfa Romeo, Fiat, Delage, and Talbot, leaving only Bugatti and Maserati to operate teams of their own as well as building cars for privateers. Many events calling themselves grands prix simply catered for all-comers in an arrangement known as Formula Libre (literally "free formula").

So, Grover-Williams, with his smartly turned out Bugatti T35B, was precisely the kind of respectable and successful competitor Antony Noghès needed to attract to bulk out the entry list of the first Monaco Grand Prix. Maserati's factory team was a high-profile no-show; neither did Achille Varzi and Gastone Brilli-Peri deign to respond to the invitation. Still, Noghès had Rudolf Caracciola and his thunderous

7-liter Mercedes SSK. Born in Germany to Italian parents in 1901, Caracciola blended driving flair with steely indefatigability, becoming a fan favorite. For Noghès, landing this colorful character and his lively leviathan of a car was box office gold.

The Automobile Club de Monaco aimed for minimal disruption of residents' daily lives. The early hour of the practice sessions was a necessary inconvenience, since it enabled the streets to be opened to traffic for the rest of the day. Since the grid would be determined by a lottery, as was customary at the time, there was no need to shut the town off for lengthy sessions; all the competitors needed to do was familiarize themselves with the layout and finesse mechanical elements such as spring rates and gear ratios. In this era, engine performance was beginning to exceed the capabilities of the rickety ladder-frame chassis, skinny tires, and cable-operated drum brakes to contain it: Grover-Williams's Bugatti could hit 60 miles per hour in around six seconds, but guiding it around corners and prevailing upon it to slow down demanded guts and feel.

Pavements were blocked with fences and hoardings to encourage spectators to buy tickets to the viewing enclosures and, naturally, a bookmakers' stall (owned by the state-sanctioned monopoly, of course) opened outside the casino. Bugattis of various vintages and engine displacements dominated the sixteen-car grid, which included five cars running in the supercharged 1.5-liter voiturette class. Among the Bugatti drivers was René Dreyfus in a 1.5-liter T37, another last-minute entrant who had been given a pass on account of his track record and his friendship with Chiron.

The lottery placed Grover-Williams, in his British racing green–liveried 2.3-liter T35, in the middle of the second row of the grid behind three 2-liter T35s. Caracciola was drawn on the fifth row and not expected to make much progress in his relatively cumbersome beast.

Grover-Williams snatched the lead on the first lap, and, remarkably, it was Caracciola who led the pursuit, flinging the white Mercedes around the streets as if the lampposts, curbs, cliffs, and brick walls didn't exist. They disputed the lead throughout— sheer grunt versus agility—and for Caracciola, a heart-in-mouth moment every time he arrived at the gasometer and station hairpins at full chat. A farcical pitstop at half distance in which his jack slipped down a tramway rail and his wheel hammer lost its handle put Caracciola a lap and a quarter down, but he fought back to third place by the time race director Charles Faroux waved the checkered flag. The race had lasted nearly four hours.

Today a sculpture at the Place Sainte-Dévote commemorates Grover-Williams's victory. He married Aubicq in November 1929 and raced to further successes, notably the brutal ten-hour Belgian Grand Prix of 1931, before heading for what he hoped would be a quiet retirement in the French country-side in 1933.

The coming of war changed all that. Grover-Williams returned to the UK and enlisted for service, initially as a driver, but his manifest resource-fulness and linguistic fluency brought him to the attention of the Special Operations Executive, a se-cret force established by the British government to perform espionage, counterintelligence, and sabo-tage operations against axis forces. Parachuted back into France under the code name Vladimir, Grover-Williams set up his own intelligence network, operating with fellow grand prix drivers Robert Benoist and Jean-Pierre Wimille.

Grover-Williams and Benoist were compromised and captured in July 1943, and while Benoist escaped—though he would be caught again and murdered in captivity—Grover-Williams was tortured and interned in Sachsenhausen concentration camp, where he was executed by firing squad in March 1945.

Or was he?

The supposed second life of William Grover-Williams requires a certain suspension of disbelief. Although the Nazis were peculiarly assidu-ous in documenting the minutiae of their murderous regime, even they stopped short of committing the full horror of the concentration camps to paper. Word went around in rac-ing circles in the 1950s claiming that someone was signing auto-graphs at events as "W Williams," but there is nothing to substantiate these claims. As to Georges Tambal, the man who moved in with Yvonne Aubicq in 1948 and allegedly shared a birthday with Grover-Williams as well as a certain mechanical apti-tude, little but anecdotal evidence remains. After Aubicq's death in 1973, Tambal moved to Agen, where he met his maker ten years later in a bicycle accident. The trail is cold.

CHAPTER FOUR

RACING AGAINST THE REICH

IN THE SHADOW OF WAR

For the wealthy, Monaco was isolated from but not immune to the creeping social, economic, and cultural changes running in the vanguard of war. Throughout the 1920s, the roulette wheels had carried on spinning and the dance floors had rumbled to the rhythmic pounding of finely tailored shoes as economies worldwide boomed or busted. In America, fortunes turned on rampant property and stock market speculation; in Germany, runaway inflation debauched the currency such that citizens were forced to collect their wages in suitcases and wheelbarrows, and the deflation that followed was equally catastrophic. In Monaco, the champagne continued to flow as Wall Street crashed and the Nazis rose to power.

But the principality was moving gently with the times, as evinced by architectural details that are even now passing into history as twenty-first-century Monaco repurposes its own real estate. Today, if you were to stroll below the iconic stone balustrades bordering the curve of the Rue de la Piscine at Tabac, or climb up the hill and take in the magnificently ornate frontages of the casino and the Hôtel Hermitage, you might think that Monaco spent the first half of the twentieth century locked in a Belle Époque bubble. Many of the elegant villas dating from this era have long since been demolished to make way for high-rise apartments, but the transition from Belle Époque architecture to postwar utilitarianism wasn't instant and seamless.

Designed by the architect and writer Charles Letrosne, the Sporting d'Hiver opened in 1932 on what had been the site of the Palais des Beaux-Arts, a building as grandiose as its title suggested, built in 1893 as part of the wider development around the casino and Hôtel de Paris. The metal-framed glass roof of the Palais called to mind the magnificence of Paxton's Crystal Palace in London; the incongruous austerity of the square-edged Sporting d'Hiver must have presented a shocking contrast. It was an early example of Monaco unmaking its past and rebuilding itself in its contemporary image. What had been an ornate indoor garden for exotic plants, flanked by a ballroom and an art gallery, was replaced by an enclosure for purely profit-driven enterprises: gaming rooms, a restaurant, a nightclub, and meeting spaces, wrapped in the ambience of a London-style private members' club. Later in its life, it would become

the offices of the Société des Bains de Mer, the monopoly that sprang from the joint-venture company formed by the Grimaldis and outside investors in the previous century.

The world of elite motor racing, which visited Monaco once a year, was also taking baby steps towards modernity. Antony Noghès's triumph in the early years of the Monaco Grand Prix was to attract a consistently high-quality field against the background of a racing scene in continuous tumult. Year on year, the network of auto clubs that sought to govern world motor racing tried and failed to conjure a set of regulations that would sufficiently titillate competitors, promoters, and the paying public alike. Twenty-first-century readers will naturally associate "grand prix" with the modern Formula 1 world championship, whereas in this era that title generally denoted a mixed-machinery race in which a substantial prize purse awaited the winners. At 100,000 francs, the prize for coming in first at Monaco dwarfed most others, especially in the austerity era.

Watching the likes of Caracciola's gargantuan Mercedes SSK uneasily cohabiting the narrow streets with grand prix machinery kept the race-goers of Monaco sufficiently entertained for several seasons before the stars aligned for a universally agreed-upon competition. A rules package manufacturers

could work with—a maximum "dry" car weight of 750 kilograms and a minimum body cross-section at the driver's seat of 33.5×9.9 inches, but otherwise anything goes—provided one spur to the remarkable spurt of technical excellence that followed in the 1930s. State aid—by fascist governments—furnished another.

The first five Monaco Grands Prix remained happily out of step with the governing body's regulatory gyrations, including the bizarre stipulation from 1931 to 33 that grands prix last between five and ten hours. Three hours on the streets of the principality were enough of a test of strength and fortitude, and if the field sometimes lacked variety, the racing compensated in other ways: in 1931, when sixteen of the twenty-eight entries were Bugattis and Caracciola had to retire his Mercedes early, the indefatigable Luigi Fagioli plugged on gamely in his over-geared Maserati to challenge the eventual winner, home favorite Louis Chiron.

The AIACR governing body arrived at the 750-kilogram formula in consultation with industry experts, including Dr. Ferdinand Porsche, who had masterminded several Mercedes racing machines in the 1920s. But, although the new formula was flagged up well in advance, much changed elsewhere in the

world between its announcement in 1932 and its debut in 1934. Hitler's National Socialists rose to power and sought to jump-start the moribund German economy with—among other policies—a program of national motorization with state-subsidized grand prix activities at its figurehead.

If the original idea had been to have one manufacturer flying the German flag, factional infighting resulted in two: Mercedes and Auto Union (a newly incorporated amalgamation of Audi, DKW, Horch, and Wanderer), one fielding a conventional front-engined machine, the other entering a radical Porsche-designed chassis with a rear-mounted V-16 engine. On April 2, 1934, the sixth Monaco signaled both a beginning and an end: it was the first major event to run under the new formula, but because the German cars were not yet ready for competition, the field consisted entirely of older cars modified to meet the new regulations. Solutions to that differed: Enzo Ferrari's Alfa Romeos were rebodied around the cockpit to meet the new width requirements; Bugatti fitted supplementary panels to add two inches to the cockpit width, but the T59s were overweight and required metal to be drilled out elsewhere.

The 750-kilogram maximum weight formula was intended to rein in the excesses of Formula Libre racing, perhaps the most egregious example of which was the twin-engined Alfa Romeo Tipo A. As with many subsequent attempts to cap performance down the years, there were unintended consequences. With the Nazi government channeling subsidies to Mercedes and Auto Union in Germany, and Benito Mussolini doing likewise with Alfa Romeo in Italy, car performance radically increased—beyond the ability of many established manufacturers to keep up, given the distorted economies of Europe at the time.

So, the 1934 Monaco was a joyous microcosm. Chiron, in a red Alfa, had the race utterly under control, routing even the mighty Tazio Nuvolari. Achille Varzi, another pre-race favorite, lost time to a long pit stop, and contemporary reports claimed he cruised to the finish smoking a cigar. With two laps to run, Chiron out-braked himself at the station hairpin and embedded his P3 in the sandbags, enabling his young Algerian-born teammate, Guillaume "Guy" Moll, to snatch the lead and win by a minute. It was to be the high point of the promising Moll's short career: he lost his life in a fatal accident later that year.

From now on, until the outset of war, things would be very different.

PRINT THE LEGEND

> **"THE CARS HAD NEVER BEEN PAINTED WHITE, SO THERE WAS NO PAINT TO GRIND OFF."**
>
> **—EUGEN REICHLE, MERCEDES MECHANIC**

Until the controversial advent of title sponsorship in the 1960s, cars predominantly raced in the national colors of their entrant: deep green for Britain, flamboyant blue for France, *rosso corsa* for Italy, vivid yellow for Belgium . . . but in the 1930s, German cars, having raced in plain white, began presenting themselves in silver. Even before they began to dominate the Monaco Grand Prix during the mid-1930s, they had acquired a nickname: the Silver Arrows.

The reasons for this are shrouded in a delightful—but recently debunked—myth. The central figure of this yarn is Alfred Neubauer, a characterful individual of Hitchcockian stature who served as Mercedes's racing manager until the marque quit motor racing in 1955. Neubauer's memoir, *Männer, Frauen und Motoren* published in English as *Speed Was My Life*, recounts the troubled genesis of the Mercedes W25 in May 1934: in its first scheduled race, a 183-mile blast around the part-banked Avus speed-bowl near Berlin, all three examples had to be withdrawn when the highly volatile fuel mix began corroding the pipes. After this ignominy—and the fact that Guy Moll won the Avus race in an Alfa Romeo—no further failures could be tolerated lest Herr Hitler began to chafe. So, when the three works W25s were found to be overweight at Mercedes's next race, the Eifelrennen at the Nürburgring, Neubauer dictated that the team should scrub off the white paint and race the cars in bare metal, literally scraping under the weight limit.

Thus the spectators at the Nürburgring were thrilled by the sight and sound of the svelte silver cars and their screaming supercharged 3.7-liter straight-eight engines roaring through the rolling Eifel forest. Manfred von Brauchitsch took a

hugely popular home victory. "And so silver replaced white as the German national racing color—the Silver Arrows had been born," concluded Neubauer triumphantly. The story even found its way into the official canon promulgated by Mercedes-Benz itself.

New evidence came to light during the 1990s that forced the company to reexamine its own history. Although a number of contemporary witnesses—including Brauchitsch himself—had repeated Neubauer's story, Mercedes's own press release announcing the car in March 1934 had described it as "ein silberne Pfeil" (a silvered arrow). A trackside radio commentary recorded at Avus in May 1932 included the commentator's description of Brauchitsch's Mercedes SSKL as "der silberne Pfeil." A Mercedes mechanic from the era confirmed that the W25 had been silver all along, and photographs of it in practice for the abortive Avus race backed this up.

There were also the inescapable facts that the Auto Unions had been racing in silver all along, and that the Eifelrennen was a Formula Libre event, so the Mercedes W25 would have been eligible to race irrespective of its weight.

Whatever, silver would be the color of the cars that dominated the Monaco Grand Prix until war overtook Europe.

IF YOU CAN'T BEAT THEM, JOIN THEM

Easter Monday, April 22, 1935. A curious and febrile atmosphere hung in the air as Monaco prepared for what would be the first race of the new seven-race European Championship. It should have been an occasion for celebration: for years now the association of auto clubs that governed motorsports had been searching for a mutually agreeable technical formula that would enable more than a handful of grands prix across the continent to coalesce into a championship.

And yet that very continent was now drifting towards war. Over the preceding two years, Adolf Hitler's National Socialist party had routed its political opponents in Germany and consolidated its grip on power, elevating Hitler not only to the position of chancellor but also, through the Enabling Act of 1933, effectively the head of a dictatorship. Riding a populist wave of resentment at the economic effects of Germany's post–World War I suppression, and scapegoating outgroups such as communists and Jews, Hitler set about undoing the postwar settlement. He withdrew from the League of Nations, presided over a highly dubious referendum in which the Saar Basin—split off from Germany after World War I and administered

by the League of Nations—voted by a 90 percent majority to be returned to Germany, and established an air force, the *Luftwaffe*. Just over a month before the Monaco Grand Prix, Hitler had announced a huge program of conscription that would bring the German army to over six times the size permitted by the Treaty of Versailles.

So, it was hardly surprising that as the three silver Mercedes W125s arrived on the front row of the grid, the streets echoed to the boos and jeers of the spectators crammed into the grandstands, pressing up against the barriers and hanging out of the windows. The noisy berating only dissipated with the arrival of crowd favorites Tazio Nuvolari and René Dreyfus onto the second row in their red Scuderia Ferrari-entered Alfa Romeos, with teammate Louis Chiron in the middle of the row behind. Politics, as ever, was selective when favorites were concerned: Nuvolari owed his place in the Ferrari team to the insistence of the Italian fascist dictator Benito Mussolini.

As the organizers hoisted the national flags of all the entrants, German visitors noted that they had chosen to raise the nation's former black, red, and yellow stripes rather than the newly instituted red flag with a black swastika inset in a white circle. The sun, according to contemporary reports, struggled to peek through darkly pendulous clouds.

Nevertheless, this race was Mercedes's to lose. Auto Union had declined to enter, thinking the wheelbase of their mid-engined V16 monsters too long for the circuit's tight corners, and, over the past year, most grands prix had fallen to one of the silver cars, provided they ran reliably. Their principal point of weakness was the braking system, for these were the early days of hydraulic rather than cable-operated brakes, but it was the same for their rivals. Scuderia Ferrari's Alfa Romeos arrived at Monaco with bigger engines than before and independent suspension, but were still shown the way during practice. Rudolf Caracciola's pole position time was nearly three seconds faster than Nuvolari and Dreyfus could manage, and nearly two seconds faster than the 1934 pole time set by Carlo Felice Trossi in an Alfa TipoB/P3, though the comparison isn't rigorous since the chicane was moved for 1935 and some corners reprofiled to eliminate adverse camber.

As the race unfolded, cheers greeted every misfortune that afflicted Mercedes: Manfred van Brauchitsch retired at the end of the first lap, and while Luigi Fagioli stretched into the lead, Caracciola—still not quite the driver he was before his huge crash in 1933—came under spirited attack from Dreyfus and the Maserati of Philippe Étancelin before a failed valve ruled the Mercedes out. Brake problems afflicted all the Alfas—and Étancelin's Maserati—but it was lack of fuel that forced Chiron to halt temporarily three laps from the end while running nearly five minutes behind Fagioli. His own fans whistled and jeered in frustration.

Fagioli crossed the finishing line thirty-one seconds ahead of Dreyfus after one hundred laps, bagging the top prize of 100,000 francs for Mercedes, as well as a 10,000 reichsmark win dividend from the German government's coffers. Only eight of the fifteen starters were classified at the finish: one Mercedes, four Alfas, and three Maseratis. Just one Bugatti started the race, and that one in British racing green (driven by Earl Howe), since finance had forced Bugatti to shelve its race efforts. Tellingly, Fagioli completed the distance eight minutes faster than Guy Moll's winning time from 1934. In all respects, the silver cars were leaving their rivals behind.

Perhaps it's not surprising, then, that racing drivers hungry for success at all costs set aside what reservations they might have had about aligning themselves with flag bearers for unsavory regimes. For 1936, Louis Chiron joined Mercedes, and the Nazi flags were displayed alongside the German cars on the grid at Monaco, where Chiron demonstrated his local knowledge and skill by qualifying on pole position.

By early 1936, fascist government–backed entrants had all but eliminated factory competition from other marques. Maserati remained on the fringes but could scarcely afford to develop its cars and was destined to withdraw at the end of the season; Bugatti was already a receding speck in the rearview mirror. The 750-kilogram formula was out of control and the governing body knew it, casting about for new proposals that could be brought into force quickly—but no consensus could be achieved until October. Meanwhile, Mercedes had developed a new 5.6-liter supercharged V-12 to replace the 4.3-liter straight eight, which entailed cutting the W25's wheelbase in order to come under the weight limit; Auto Union brought the C-type's thirty-two-valve midmounted V-16 lump from 4.4 to 6 liters, a staggering increase for a car that was already capable of breaking traction at well over 100 miles per hour.

The Spanish Civil War had begun. Italian forces had invaded Abyssinia. Hitler had deployed the German

army in the Rhineland, once again thumbing his nose at the Treaty of Versailles, and set about dismantling the civil rights of German Jews. And yet, on Easter Monday in 1936, barely a chirrup of protest greeted Chiron's appearance at the wheel of a Mercedes on the Monaco grid.

Mercedes reverted to the straight-eight engine for Monaco and yet Chiron had outpaced all four Auto Unions. The rear-engined cars were appearing for the first time in the principality, and so were three of their four drivers: Hans Stuck, Ernst von Delius, Bernd Rosemeyer, and Achille Varzi. Nuvolari's 3.8-liter Alfa and Caracciola's Mercedes joined Chiron on the front row, but rain and a catastrophic oil leak on one of the Alfas would lend a note of farce to the opening laps.

The leak on Antonio Brivio's Scuderia Ferrari Alfa was noticed before the start, but the team simply ordered him to swap cars with Monaco first-timer Mario Tadini. Last away from the grid, Tadini's 8C-35 deposited the contents of its sump on the wet track before expiring at the end of the first lap, causing a hairy moment at the chicane as the leaders came through on the following tour. The fast-starting Caracciola and Nuvolari had already lapped Tadini's stuttering Alfa just before the chicane; Chiron arrived fully committed and slid off into the sandbags. Some of the

following drivers were able to react in time, others weren't; yet the race was allowed to continue despite the remnants of three cars almost blocking the chicane. Caracciola mastered the slippery surface to win by nearly two minutes from Varzi, to great acclaim from the crowd.

Chiron's alignment with Mercedes lasted just a few months. Over the following grands prix, the company was soundly beaten by Auto Union, and after failing to cure the W25's handling issues—masked by Caracciola's finesse in Monaco—they quit before the end of the season to focus on designing an all-new car for the final year of the 750-kilogram formula. Chiron was also out of the picture by then, after injuring himself in a high-speed accident at the Nürburgring. It would be a long time before he would be seen on the streets of Monaco in a racing car again.

Car performance stretched spectator credulity even further in 1937, the final year of the 750-kilogram formula before the governing body planned to introduce new rules mirroring the American IndyCar framework, with a sliding scale of weight limits according to engine capacity (which was capped at 4.5 liters for normally aspirated engines, 3 liters for supercharged). Caracciola's pole time in the new Mercedes

W125, with a supercharged 5.7-liter straight eight, was nine seconds faster than his pole lap two years previously—albeit helped by warmer conditions since the race had been moved to August.

Extant film footage demonstrates what beasts these cars were to thread through the narrow streets, power sliding to quell terminal understeer at the station hairpin. Brauchitsch and Caracciola battled wheel-to-wheel for much of the race, Brauchitsch in open defiance of team orders to allow Caracciola through. His finishing time—a minute and a half ahead of Caracciola, who had to pit after destroying his tires trying to get past—was twenty-four minutes faster than Moll's 1934 win. The nearest non-German car was Farina's Alfa in sixth, three laps behind. Internal politics at Alfa would result in the company taking ownership of Enzo Ferrari's team and demoting him.

Racing could no longer ignore the distant rumblings of war. Against a tapestry of strikes and civil unrest across Europe, and threatening rearmament in Germany and Italy, motorsports stuttered and faded—even in the moneyed backwater of Monaco. After 1937, racing would not return to these streets until peacetime.

CHAPTER FIVE

BACK ON TRACK

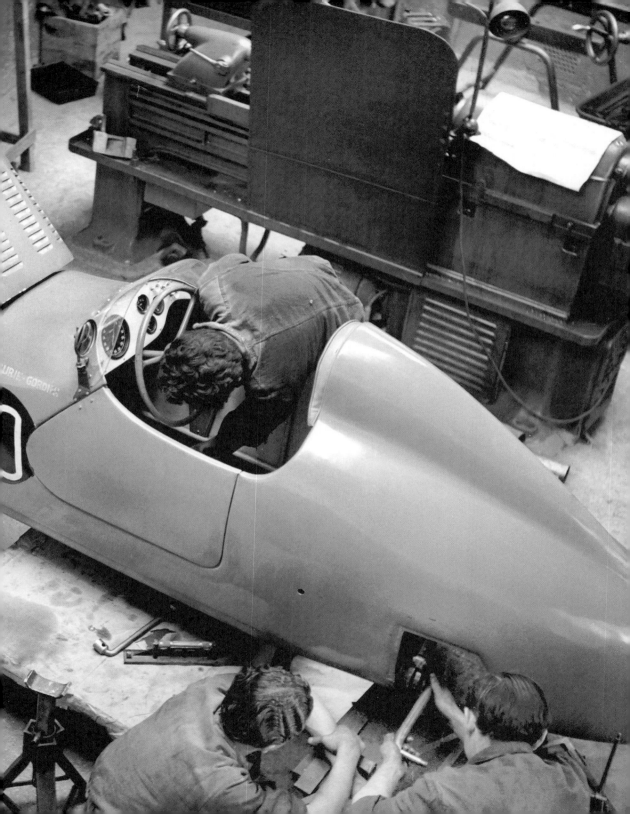

GETTING AHEAD

On September 9, 1945, something extraordinary happened. Four months after Nazi Germany's unconditional surrender, a car club held three automobile races supported by a handful of motorcycle events in the Bois de Boulogne public park in Paris. Frivolous though it might seem in retrospect, these races for cars of differing engine displacements and induction—the Coupe Robert Benoist, the Coupe de la Libération, and the Coupe des Prisonniers— were defiantly symbolic, a triumph of spirit over wherewithal. The entry was small, the cars ragtag, the circuit very basic, but as an attempt to recapture some of what had been lost to years of armed conflict, this was a significant event.

The very names of the races carried historical resonance, from the evocative generalism of "Prisoners" and "Liberation" to the specific. Robert Benoist was a national hero in two different fields, a winner of grands prix as well as the Le Mans 24 Hours and a covert Resistance operative during the war, working with fellow ex-racer (and 1929 Monaco Grand Prix winner) William Grover-Williams. Both had been captured and executed by the Nazis. Benoist had been arrested after risking a visit to Paris to see

his dying mother; the winner of the race bearing Benoist's name, Amédée Gordini, received his trophy from Benoist's daughter, and afterwards the crowd (reported to number over one hundred thousand) observed a minute's silence, broken by the trumpeters of the Parisian police playing the "Last Post."

As the European nations clawed their way out of war-enforced poverty, they faced innumerable challenges; building new racing cars did not feature highly on any country's list of priorities. And beneath the surface, the problems facing motor racing had not changed; throughout the 1930s, the grand prix scene had been, in effect, a distorted economy in which state-backed prestige projects swept aside independents. By the coming of war, even Alfa Romeo, one of those government-blessed manufacturers, had been forced to capitulate to the Germans and build cars to run in a lesser class. The rule makers of the 1930s had aspired to a world championship of top-class machinery, but now they would have to make do with whatever racing cars had survived the war.

The renamed Fédération Internationale de l'Automobile (FIA) agreed on a

rules framework initially known as Formula A, later Formula 1, defining top-class motor racing. By necessity it was informed by what already existed: cars with 1.5-liter supercharged engines, would face off against those with naturally aspirated engines no larger than 4.5 liters. What was needed now was events of sufficient standing (and financial backing) to attract such entrants as could make the journey. Monaco's return to the racing calendar in 1948 was a moment of enormous significance: here was the prewar grand prix racing scene's preeminent event returned to life.

Monaco needed the race as much as the motor racing industry needed Monaco. Like France, during the war, the principality had been forced by circumstances into committing acts justified then on grounds of expediency and duress, but whose ugliness was revealed in the unforgiving retrospective examination of peacetime. The elderly Prince Louis II had encouraged investment into Monaco by German government-backed companies during the 1930s, enabling the Nazi regime to use the principality as a financial conduit. With the onset of war, Louis suspended the constitution and ruled the increasingly divided state—by decree.

By late 1940, with much of France under German occupation and the collaborationist Vichy government presiding over the rest, Louis's hopes of keeping Monaco out of the war were already fading. The principality was occupied by Italian forces, then by Germans, allowing itself to be used as a recreational center for troops and a money laundry by Nazi grandees. Louis duly aligned himself with France's Vichy regime under his old army colleague Marshal Pétain and capitulated to a German dictate compelling him to register all Jewish citizens.

For many years, official accounts of Monaco's history liked to claim that the principality was not party to the outrages of Nazism. But while Louis did act to protect several prominent Jewish citizens, including Édouard de Rothschild, the regime was complicit in the arrest and handover of a number (believed to be sixty-six) of Jewish refugees from Germany and Austria in 1944, while Monaco was under German occupation.

So, for Monaco, returning to prewar normality would not be so simple as removing the panels that had concealed the contents of the wine cellar in the Hôtel de Paris from the occupying forces and declaring business as usual. The regime was tarnished by its association with Vichy and was the subject of society scandal because Louis's adopted daughter, Princess Charlotte, the heir presumptive, had long since divorced her husband, renounced her claim to the throne, and taken up with a convicted criminal. Besides, the war years had impacted the royal coffers, which depended upon receipts from Monaco's licensed entertainments. Louis, who married the French actress Ghislaine Dommanget—twice a divorcee—in July 1946, was unmotivated to execute change at the age of seventy-six, and the couple moved to the family-owned Château de Marchais, north of Paris.

In 1929, Monaco had been described in one French newspaper as "a box of toys in which everything is brilliant and artificial and a little fragile, and must be kept carefully fitted into its place if it is not to be broken." Change—desperately needed change—was coming. In the decades to follow, Monaco would reinvent and remake itself once again, with its annual motor race acting as the centerpiece of its identity. The very ground it stood on would change. In May 1948, the Automobile Club de Monaco, led by Anthony Noghès, claimed the honor of organizing the first major "Formula A" motor race of the year. In the absence of Prince Louis II, it was the architect of Monaco's future who took a tour of the circuit with Noghès, bearing a huge flag in an open-top road car, before the start: Rainier, Louis's grandson and heir.

"RENÉ THE WALKING STICK" AND THE REMAKING OF MONACO

Monaco's postwar rehabilitation would be driven not by the elderly absentee monarch Louis II, nor by his illegitimate daughter Charlotte, but by the man who would become Prince Rainier III upon Louis's death in May 1949. Louis's legacy is complex; his wartime alignment with Vichy was questionable, and his out-of-wedlock dalliance with a proletarian had drawn ridicule. It was another thread in the tapestry of the so-called curse of the Grimaldis, requiring a constitutional amendment to preserve the family line through Charlotte via a formal adoption. Louis had spent most of his early life before he assumed the throne away from Monaco, and he left the principality shortly after the end of World War II to live with his new—and much younger—wife.

Charlotte herself was not ruler material, and after she divorced her husband, Count Pierre de Polignac (Rainier's father), and took her doctor as her lover, scandal descended upon the Grimaldis. She was prevailed upon to renounce her claim to the throne in favor of Rainier, which she did the day before his twenty-first birthday. Even then, Charlotte could not fade quietly into the background; after Louis's death, she moved into the Château de Marchais and converted it into a rehabilitation center for convicted criminals—one of whom, the notorious jewel thief René Girier, she took as a lover.

Girier was a larger-than-life character with gentlemanly affectations. His long criminal career began before the war, during which he was captured by the Gestapo and shot while attempting escape. Thereafter, he walked with a limp and used a cane, which, as his reputation grew, earned him the nickname René la Canne—René the Walking Stick. He had already escaped from jail eleven times when he fell into Charlotte's orbit.

Rainier, who became the sovereign prince upon Louis's death in May 1949, gave Monaco's monarchy a much-needed reputational facelift. Born in the principality in 1923, he was sent to another country to study after his parents divorced. Initially he was educated in England, first at Summerfields near Hastings and then at Stowe. He loathed Stowe and his parents relocated him to less austere surroundings in Switzerland.

Three months after becoming the anointed heir to the throne at the age of twenty-one, he enlisted as a volunteer in the French army and was subsequently decorated for bravery during the liberation of Alsace-Lorraine. When he succeeded Louis in 1949, Rainier grasped a universal truth that had eluded his father: the people love royalty. Though he was not especially garrulous, Rainier made a point of being *seen*.

He had to work quickly. Monaco might have rebooted its annual Grand Prix in 1948, but in 1949 the event had to be cancelled. The royal coffers were running dry; in the last year of the decade, visitors to the casino fell by 90 percent compared with its prewar peak. Culture was moving on, leaving stuffy and ragged Monaco behind.

Rainier's strategy was to rebuild Monaco from the ground up, diversifying away from the casino and focusing on tourism, light industry, and finance. But to do that, he would require investment. He tried and failed to persuade American investors to buy into the casino and build new hotels. Like a shark sensing blood, Greek shipping magnate Aristotle Onassis began to acquire a majority stake in SBM through

proxy buyers in the early 1950s. Meanwhile, the French government began to chafe as they saw Rainier turning toward America, and the rancor would only grow over the following decade as Rainier welcomed French tax exiles and embarked on an ambitious if not unprecedented scheme (the harbor area had been extended in a landfill project in the nineteenth century) to extend Monaco over the sea, freeing up new real estate for development.

In time, Monaco's growth would begin to choke it with traffic. But the little Belle Époque square with its casino and the wide, tree-lined boulevards of the Grand Prix course would remain. And, beginning in 1950, the Grand Prix would become an almost permanent fixture of a new and glamorous motor racing world championship. That race would also be a debut of sorts for a competitor already well versed in wheel-to-wheel combat on the streets: Enzo Ferrari. He had spurned the first world championship grand prix at Silverstone, because the promoters wouldn't offer him enough money to field his blood-red racers. But in Monaco, he would begin an association with the sport that lasts to this day—and begin the process of trying to vanquish his former employers, Alfa Romeo.

OCEAN SPRAY

The three Fs: Fangio, Fagioli, and Farina. In 1950, Alfa Romeo Squadra Corse returned to a competitive field it had abandoned a year previously for lack of serious competition and prize money. The FIA's new world championship merited the dusting down of its remarkable 158 "voiturettes," relics of prewar racing. Spindly-tired and primitive, these scarlet creations were redolent of an era that had not yet coughed its last.

The headline entry figure of twenty-six seemed encouraging, but it barely masked motor racing's ongoing malaise: the Formula 1 regulations were just about suitable, but they belonged in a bygone era, and few manufacturers were willing to build the necessary machinery. Twenty-six became twenty-five when André Simon scratched his entry, and four other competitors failed to arrive, leaving twenty-one to qualify. Of those, a skeptical eye would have outed American playboy Harry Schell's motorcycle-engined Cooper Formula 3 car as a misfit, while over half of the remainder were prewar offerings, including the three Alfas, six Maserati 4CLTs, and two ERAs. Of the others, only the four Ferrari 125Ss and the two blue Simca-Gordini T15s entered

by prewar racer Amédée Gordini merited the tag of "new." The Talbot-Lago T26Cs were based on prewar engineering principles right down to their pushrod 4.5-liter straight-six engines, and only three of the eleven examples entered actually arrived. Ferrari's cars were much more modern and nimble, although their supercharged 1.5-liter V-12s—designed by Alfa 158 architect Gioachino Colombo—were greater on noise than dependability.

With Ferrari's young team yet to find its feet, this and subsequent grands prix would largely be duels between two fascinating protagonists. Forty-three-year-old Alfa Romeo team leader Giuseppe Farina was of that generation who had lost many of his prime racing years to the war and carried a reputation for physical, elbows-out racing that some called reckless. Argentine Juan Manuel Fangio, five years his junior, scarcely seemed a racing driver at all with his unglamorous bearing and bow-legged stance. And yet, behind the wheel, he balanced aggression and circumspection exquisitely, and his star was very much on the rise. Fangio put his 158 on pole at Monaco in a time of one minute 50.2 seconds, a little under three seconds off Rudolf Caracciola's 1937

benchmark but 2.6 seconds faster than teammate Farina. Anecdotal history has it that during a drinks reception hosted by the Automobile Club de Monaco, Fangio perused the assembled memorabilia with great interest, his eyes alighting for a long time on a picture of the second-lap crash in 1936 in which several drivers, including Farina, spun off on oil at the chicane.

History would repeat itself to some degree on race day when seawater from the harbor splashed over the balustrade at Tabac, a sharp left-hander that twenty-first-century F1 drivers tackle with but a brief feathering of the throttle. Fangio had been preoccupied with the threat of Farina; it would be crucial not only to stay ahead of him at the start, but to establish enough of a gap to dissuade Farina from trying anything foolish. But Fangio's chief threat would not come from the front row of the grid, nor the second.

As was customary at the time, the grid was laid out in an alternating 3-2-3-2 pattern. The first five positions, with the Maserati of Fangio's countryman José Froilán González completing the front row and pre-war hero Philippe Étancelin's Talbot Lago alongside Luigi Fagioli's Alfa on the second, were set after Thursday's practice session. The remainder were established on Saturday, when

Ferrari's Luigi Villoresi posted a lap of one minute 52.3 seconds—which would have put him alongside Fangio had he set it two days previously. Instead he was on row three with teammate Alberto Ascari and the recently unretired fifty-year-old Louis Chiron.

At forty-one, Villoresi had emerged from the domestic rallying scene in the mid-1930s alongside younger brother Emilio, whom some considered the more gifted of the two—enough for Enzo Ferrari to recruit him to race in grands prix for the factory Alfa Romeo team. But Emilio was killed in June 1939 while testing one of the then-new Alfa Romeos and Luigi had been appalled by Enzo's standoffish attitude in the aftermath. Luigi had been forbidden to even see the wreckage, then informed that there was no insurance. He had accepted Enzo's offer of a drive in late 1949 only after much soul-searching, and with the proviso that Enzo would also employ Ascari, Luigi's friend and protégé.

On the morning of May 21, race day, a stiff wind blew in from the sea, snapping sharply at the starter's flag as it dropped. The roar of engines large and small filled the air amid the screech of skinny tires pawing at the asphalt. Farina nosed ahead of Fangio as they bore down upon the first corner, a hairpin, with the ugly

iron gasometer beyond. Villoresi, rocketing ahead of Chiron and Ascari and past Étancelin, Fagioli, and González, latched on to Fangio's tail and followed him through as Fangio surged past Farina up the tree-lined hill towards Casino Square.

As the field roared back down the hill towards the demanding hairpin by the station, then to the claustrophobic blast through the tunnel and back towards the harbor, the wind whipped up a series of waves that crashed over the harborside and onto the road at Tabac. Fangio, perhaps carrying that image of 1936 in the back of his mind, drifted skillfully through the corner, as did Villoresi. Farina, following, sawed at his Alfa's huge wood-rimmed steering wheel to no avail as his car slithered off and crashed into the stone steps beyond, rebounding back into the path of Fagioli, who threw his Alfa sideways in a futile effort to avoid his team leader. The two cars were briefly interlocked until González struck and parted them, somehow contriving to keep his Maserati rolling on. Chiron, Raymond Sommer, and Ascari skillfully dodged through the gap González had created, but as the marshals went into a panic and directed Louis Rosier to bring his Talbot Lago to a halt, the drivers behind were too slow to react to the stationary car and slammed into it.

In all, nine cars were eliminated on the opening lap, and González would only manage one more before the contents of his leaking fuel tank ignited, forcing him to abandon his post. Tabac was a lake of seawater and fuel from the crashed cars. Nevertheless, amid the chaos and poor communication, the race went on. Fangio ticked off another lap, but as he rocketed out of the tunnel and braked for the chicane, he realized something was amiss.

"I could detect agitation among the spectators," he said later. "They were not looking at me leading the race, but were looking the other way."

Slowing down well in advance of Tabac and raising an arm to caution his pursuers to follow his example, Fangio arrived to find the road blocked by smashed race cars and scurrying marshals. Pulling alongside one of the wrecks, Fangio reached out and shoved it, creating just enough of a gap to drive through. Behind, Villoresi stalled his Ferrari. It would not be his day after all.

Fangio cantered to victory with a lap in hand over Ascari, who in turn was a lap ahead of Chiron. It took three hours and thirteen minutes for the winner to complete one hundred laps, and only six other cars were running at the finish.

It was the first world championship victory for the man who would go on to claim motor racing's ultimate prize five times. But it would be five years before Fangio would race a Formula 1 car at Monaco again and seven before he won there. The Grand Prix was cancelled in 1951 and run as an event for sports cars in 1952, with a smaller prize pot.

Prince Rainier was an undoubted car nut, and he well knew the value of holding the Grand Prix, but during this period, other matters consumed his attention: the principality's parlous financial state, his grand plan to alter the balance of the economy and reclaim land from the sea, and his need to find a suitable wife and secure the succession. This latter element became still more pressing when it became known that his elder sister Antoinette was supposedly scheming to have the constitution amended so that her son Christian replace or succeed him. There were also the plots of Aristotle Onassis to untangle once he had established a majority shareholding of SBM and, in effect, become a rival head of state. Rainier needed the shipping magnate's money, but he didn't need his interference. In comparison to these matters of state, a motor race, even an exciting and prestigious one, is small potatoes.

CHIRON BOWS OUT

Beyond the barriers on the driver's left as they negotiate what is now a super-fast chicane by Monaco's harborside swimming pool is a bust of a man without whose potent influence the Monaco Grand Prix might never have come into being. While race founder Anthony Noghès has a corner named after him, Louis Chiron seemingly exists on a higher plane. After the Grand Prix each May, the barriers and grandstands are taken down and the traffic-choked streets return to normal, but Chiron's bust remains.

Although his affectations made him the occasional figure of fun among drivers and journalists in his later years, Chiron was an enormously significant presence on the motor racing scene. Nobody else can claim to have been a grand prix driver for twenty-nine years.

Chiron retired before World War II, after his association with Mercedes came to an end when he crashed, injuring himself very badly, in the 1936 German Grand Prix at the Nürburgring. He *did* race again, and won the 1937 French Grand Prix in a Talbot, but then he vanished from the racing scene until after the war.

Remarkably, he took up competition again after a decade-long interregnum and won two French Grands Prix, before the FIA launched its world championship. Chiron qualified a Maserati mid-grid—5.8 seconds off the pace of polesitter Giuseppe Farina's Alfa Romeo—for the opening race at Silverstone but retired when the clutch let go after twenty-six laps. He raced in all but one of the six world championship events in 1950 and all the European grands prix in 1951. But at the beginning of 1952, he suffered severe burns when his Formula 2 Maserati caught fire during practice for a race at Syracuse and skipped the entire season, only making one-off entries thereafter.

But Chiron was determined to be on the grid when the Monaco Grand Prix returned to the Formula 1 calendar in 1955, and he obtained a seat in one of the four Lancia D50s entered by the factory. The squat short-wheelbase car was in its element on the streets, but sadly Chiron wasn't: of the twenty-three entries, only the fastest twenty would be allowed to start, and Chiron scraped through in nineteenth place. As a mark of the progress Formula 1 had made since the FIA formulated a set

of regulations to the manufacturers' liking, the top fourteen qualifiers all broke Rudolf Caracciola's eighteen-year-old lap record.

This, truly, was the year the Monaco Grand Prix recaptured past glories. On race day, under a cloudless blue sky, grandstands were creaking under the weight of paying spectators, and hotels were reportedly charging 10,000 francs for rooms with a balcony overlooking the circuit.

Chiron should perhaps have taken his cue from this, for he was out of place on a modern Formula 1 grid. While his teammates Alberto Ascari and Eugenio Castellotti were running at the front, albeit struggling to keep up with the Mercedes of Fangio and the young British charger Stirling Moss, Chiron appeared to be in a different race.

"Chiron was evidently out of his class, the new school of drivers scuttling past him when and as they liked," tut-tutted Gregor Grant in his report for *Autosport* magazine.

But Grant was almost wrong about one thing. "Chiron, absolutely all-in, was obviously delighted to feature as a finisher," he concluded after Chiron crossed the finishing line in sixth place, five laps down. "But I am afraid that this will prove to be the great Monégasque's last grand prix."

Chiron would return twice more but not make the cut, withdrawing when his Maserati 250F blew its engine in 1956 and then failing to qualify two years later at the age of fifty-eight. Thus, his racing career fizzled out as a footnote in a results sheet, but he remained indelibly associated with racing in the principality, until his death in 1979, as clerk of the course for the Monte Carlo Rally and the Monaco Grand Prix. For many years, he flagged off the field with a piece of theatre that spawned many imitators—and invited derision from some quarters.

"Hearts sunk when it was announced that Louis Chiron would give the starting signal, in honor of the fortieth anniversary of his victory at Monaco with a Bugatti," wrote Denis Jenkinson in his report of the 1971 Monaco Grand Prix for *Motor Sport* magazine.

To less churlish souls, though, Chiron would remain an indelible Monaco memory. As their heartbeats spiked in anticipation of the start, ears pounding under the assault of roaring engines, their eyes would fix upon the dapper elderly gent with the flag as he performed his time-honored routine.

CHAPTER SIX

DRIVERS AND DUELS

MOSS VS. FANGIO

In 1955, top-level motor racing returned to the streets of Monaco for the first time since 1950, in the form of a world championship Formula 1 event billed as the Grand Prix d'Europe. Monaco was on the road to prosperity again, the behind-the-scenes tussles between Prince Rainier and Aristotle Onassis notwithstanding, and F1 itself was on the mend. During Monaco's absence from the calendar, the world championship had spluttered to a virtual halt, idled for two seasons with Formula 2 cars, then roared back into life in 1954 as new technical rules attracted a host of new and returning competitors.

Chief among these were Mercedes, back at Monaco in 1955 after an eighteen-year hiatus, and presided over once again by the portly figure of Alfred Neubauer. In the context of Monaco's own faltering steps in recreating its past glories, Mercedes was to play a crucial role in re-establishing the principality's Grand Prix glamour.

The silver arrows had dominated the world championship after returning mid-season in 1954, delivering the peerless Juan Manuel Fangio to the title. And yet Neubauer

realized he was missing something. Fangio aside, Mercedes was under strength, for Karl Kling and Hans Herrmann, though of the right nationality to please the company board, lacked the final edge of pace.

"When I settled down to pick my team for 1955, I had to admit that our position was not as strong as it should be," wrote Neubauer in his autobiography, *Speed Was My Life*. "I needed a new driver, a young man. I thought of the Frenchman Jean Behra, but he had already signed on with the opposition. So I started browsing through my black notebook till I came on the name Stirling Moss."

Twenty-five years old, gifted, and in a hurry to make a name for himself, Moss had already thrown his hat into the ring for a Mercedes drive the previous year. Then, Neubauer felt he lacked top-level experience; now, after proving himself in a Maserati during 1954, Moss seemed the perfect candidate to drive alongside the great Fangio. Or was he?

"Moss tasted blood," wrote Neubauer. "His greatest ambition in life was to drive better and faster than the famous Juan Manuel Fangio. He had worked out his own plan of

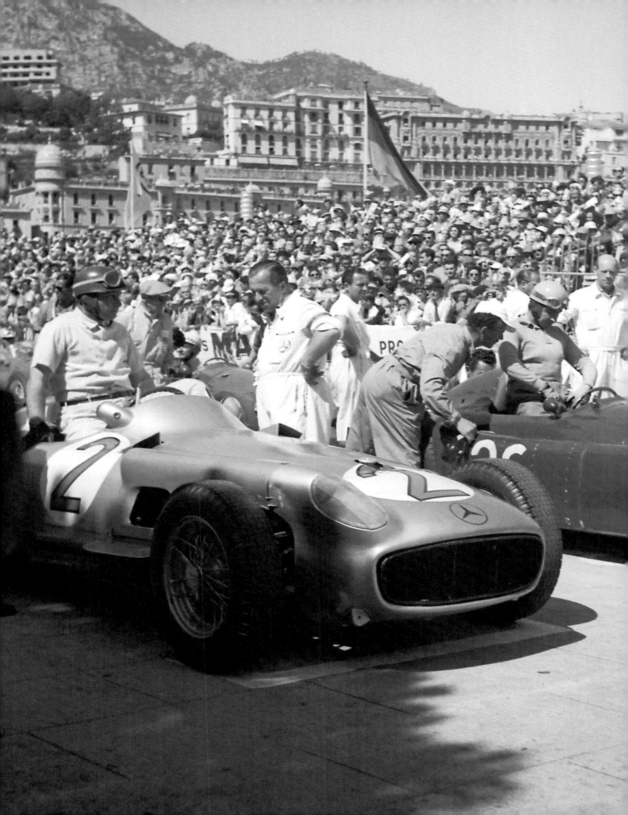

campaign, which was to get close to Fangio and stay there. Three times it went wrong."

Monaco was the second world championship race of 1955, held three months after the first, in Argentina, where Moss had been classified fourth behind the victorious Fangio, two laps down, after his own car had broken down and he took over Herrmann's. On the first day of practice, Fangio lapped five seconds under the record set by Caracciola in a Mercedes in 1937. Moss, two seconds off Fangio's pace in his own car but on par with it when he essayed a quick lap in Fangio's, recorded his frustrations in his diary, including the pitiful night's sleep that ensued.

Under a somewhat arbitrary ruling, the order of the three-car front row was determined by Friday's practice times, placing Moss on the left of the newly relocated start line on the harborside, with Fangio on the right for the inside line into the gasometer hairpin. Alberto Ascari, in the novel short-wheelbase Lancia D50 with its outboard-mounted fuel and oil tanks, was sandwiched between them and matched Fangio's pole time during practice on Saturday.

None of these three would win. After the Mercedes dispensed with Ascari's young teammate Eugenio Castellotti, who rocketed from the second row to snatch the lead briefly on the way up the hill towards the casino, Fangio led from Moss, setting a brisk enough pace for Neubauer to signal them to slow down. Neubauer would later claim that Moss was following too closely and was overcome by exhaust fumes; whether that was the case, Fangio halted with transmission failure at half distance, lap fifty, and Moss led convincingly for another thirty before his engine's sophisticated desmodromic valve system lunched itself, and he stopped in a cloud of oil smoke. Ascari, perhaps distracted by the suddenly animated crowd or taken unawares by the oil trail from Moss's car, then speared through the straw bales at the chicane and plunged into the harbor. As if to prove that sometimes Monaco can be as random as a spin of the roulette wheel, Maurice Trintignant, driving an elderly and unfancied ex-F2 Ferrari chassis, was the surprised beneficiary.

Still, this had been a memorable and fascinating race, and one that inked Monaco into the sporting consciousness as a place of high drama once again. Sadly, dramas elsewhere conspired against a repeat of this three-way duel for victory the following season: four days later, Ascari crashed fatally while testing a Ferrari sportscar, and Mercedes was involved in the accident that killed eighty-three spectators in the annual sports car enduro at Le Mans,

prompting four grands prix to be cancelled and Mercedes to withdraw from motor racing at the end of the season. Of the six F1 races that counted to the world championship, Fangio won four, Moss one.

So, in 1956, Moss and Fangio would be rivals once more, but teammates no longer. Moss, the 1955 championship runner-up, returned to the Maserati fold while Fangio sought refuge at Ferrari, who had grudgingly taken on the moribund Lancia team's superior D50 cars. But, for the world champion, this was an unhappy arrangement, since Enzo Ferrari—the self-confessed "agitator of men"—refused to enshrine Fangio as the team number one.

Still, Fangio was able to take over the car of teammate Luigi Musso in Argentina when his own broke down, as was the customary right of the team leader, so status anxiety cannot completely explain his out-of-sorts performance at Monaco four months later. Fangio qualified on pole, with Moss's Maserati and Castellotti's Ferrari-Lancia alongside on the front row. But Moss took the lead and by the end of the first lap was five seconds ahead.

The layout of the chicane had been amended to avoid a repeat of Ascari's aquatic adventure, but it remained challenging, and on the second lap

Fangio spun and deranged the hay-bales, causing two other drivers to crash out. Fangio charged back into contention, helped by Castellotti's retirement and team-mate Peter Collins moving over to let him back into second place, but on the thirty-second lap he made a mess of the chicane again and clipped the wall with a rear wheel. Seemingly spent, he pitted and let Castellotti take the car over once it had been repaired.

For a full twenty-two laps, Fangio brooded in the pits. Then, when Collins brought his car in, Fangio decided to rejoin. Collins had been running in second place before his stop, and now Fangio had a forty-five-second gap to make up. It was a tall order, and yet the revitalized champion threw his team-mate's Ferrari-Lancia around Monaco's confines with confidence and skill. Moss, nursing a car damaged in contact with a tail-ender, was a relieved man as he crossed the finishing line just over six seconds ahead.

Unfortunately for Moss, he would win just one more grand prix this season. But for his country's imperial misadventure in Suez, which triggered an oil crisis that in turn led to two world championship races being cancelled, he might have

had further opportunities to score under F1's abstruse points system of the time in which only a driver's five best scores counted. He finished just three points short of Fangio, who owed his title to the selflessness of Collins, who once again handed his car over at the final round after Musso had refused to do so.

1957 was the final year in which Moss and Fangio would face off against one another on the streets of Monaco, and on paper this was a promising contest. Fangio decided the Maserati's aging 250F was a better bet than Ferrari's decreasingly effective developments to the ex-Lancia D50s; Moss drove a 250F in Argentina before swapping horses to Vanwall, a British marque very much on the up. In Monaco Fangio tried Maserati's new V12 engine in practice before electing to stay with the tried-and-trusted inline six. In this race, guile as well as speed would deliver him the win.

Fangio qualified his Maserati on pole, but he was most concerned by his company there: not only Moss, but a host of other young British hopefuls eager to make their mark. His former teammate Collins was next to him on the grid in a Ferrari, Moss completing the front row on the left-hand side. Immediately behind were Moss's teammate Tony

Brooks, and the devil-may-care Mike Hawthorn in another Ferrari. Just as he had in 1950, Fangio made a silent resolution not to get caught up in any first-lap foolishness.

When the starter's flag dropped, Fangio allowed Moss and Collins to roar off into a duel for the lead while he kept Brooks and Hawthorn at arm's length. On the fourth time around, Moss badly misjudged the chicane and crashed through the straw bales and sandbags, scattering detritus all about. Collins had no time to react and slammed into the guardrails over-looking the harbor. Fangio threaded his way through with finesse as Brooks braked sharply, taking Hawthorn un-awares. For the rest of the race, the Ferraris of Collins and Hawthorn re-mained parked almost one on top of the other. Moss trudged back to the pits on foot, and Fangio controlled the pace up front to win by twenty-five seconds from Brooks.

Moss won three grands prix—one shared with Brooks—but it was still not enough to prevent Fangio from re-cording his fifth world title. It would be nearly half a century before any-one matched this feat. Moss was nearly the man once again, and when Fangio elected to contest the Indy 500 in 1958, then retire from racing, it brought this particular chapter of F1 history to a close.

MOSS VS. THE FERRARIS

For safety reasons and to dissuade time wasters, right up until the 1970s, grid numbers at Monaco were usually capped at an arbitrary (and often hotly contested) figure. In 1957, that number had been sixteen, and although one of the curious little British Cooper cars with the diminutive rear-mounted, 2-liter straight-four Climax engines had failed to make the grade, the other one qualified fifteenth. Its driver, a young Australian called Jack Brabham, got as high as third before running out of fuel—luckily for him at the top of the hill by the casino, enabling him to coast down and then push the car home. The following year, Stirling Moss won the opening round in Argentina in the same car.

At the time, the first world championship victory for a rear-engined car was viewed as a quirk of fate rather than a pivotal moment in the sport's history. But when Maurice Trintignant won the Monaco Grand Prix four months later in a new Cooper chassis, beating Luigi Musso's Ferrari by twenty seconds, it proved decisively that, on some courses, agility could trump outright power.

Enzo Ferrari disparaged the new generation of predominantly British-based teams and chassis builders as "garagistes," but rear-engined cars quickly became de rigueur. By 1961, even Ferrari was forced to run up the white flag and place the engine behind the driver, having been routed by the likes of Cooper and Lotus.

Moss claimed Lotus's first world championship victory at Monaco in 1960, but such were the performance gains of the new generation

> **"IF I'D REPEATED MY POLE POSITION TIME ON EVERY ONE OF THOSE 100 LAPS, I'D ONLY HAVE BEATEN MYSELF BY ABOUT 40 SECONDS. THAT UNDERLINES HOW HARD I HAD TO DRIVE."**
>
> **—STIRLING MOSS**

of cars that the governing body felt it prudent to step in. For 1961, they declared, F1 engines would be capped at 1.5 liters, naturally aspirated. Ferrari already had an F2 engine of suitable displacement on the dyno, a compact V-6 producing nearly 200 brake horsepower. But the British teams pushed back vigorously, filing protests that would ultimately prove fruitless. Had they ploughed that time into engine development, the 1961 season might have turned out rather differently.

Brabham had won the world championship in 1959 and 1960 with Cooper, but in sleeved-down 1.5-liter form, the Climax four-cylinder engine lacked grunt compared with Ferrari's more sophisticated V-6. Brabham would finish just two grands prix in 1961.

Monaco that year, the first race of the season, was a thrilling aberration thanks to Moss's brilliance. He wasn't even in the latest Lotus, preferring to drive an older one entered by Rob Walker Racing, a team he trusted to screw the car together properly (Lotus had a reputation for fragility, and Moss had broken both legs when a wheel fell off his car at high speed during practice for the 1960 Belgian GP).

Moss qualified on pole—albeit nearly three seconds off his 1960 pole time—ahead of the new Ferrari of Richie Ginther, with Jim Clark in the new works Lotus completing the front row.

As Louis Chiron toured the course in an immaculate blue Citroën DS19 ahead of the race start, perhaps he might have recalled his own racing exploits against theoretically superior machinery thirty years previously. Moss had outqualified cars to which his Climax engine was giving away at least 30 brake horsepower. As Chiron brandished his starter's flag with his usual theatre, Ginther made a crisp getaway to lead into the gasometer hairpin, and Clark eased the British racing green Lotus ahead of Moss's squarer, stubbier, deep-blue one, chased by Jo Bonnier in the silver Porsche.

A stuttering fuel pump soon forced Clark to pit, and Moss dug in to chase and pass Ginther on the fourteenth lap, carrying Bonnier with him. Ginther's teammate Phil Hill also came through, passing Bonnier for second on lap twenty-four, and when the Porsche began to fall back, Ginther went by and closed up on his teammate.

It was a stultifyingly hot day—enough for Moss to have asked for the non-structural side panels of his car to be removed to let more air into the cockpit—and yet he seemed unruffled as he kept the Ferraris at bay. Every time he exited the hairpin outside the railway station, he glanced upwards at the red cars in pursuit. Moss just looked

at where they were in relation to the lampposts compared with the last lap and logged that as a measure of how hard he had to push—and what level of risk he had to take passing tail-enders—to maintain the gap. Frustrated at seeing Moss continuously dancing out of reach, Ferrari team manager Romolo Tavoni signaled his drivers to swap places at mid-distance so that Ginther, the only one of the three with the new 120-degree V-6, could push again. Ginther duly gave it everything, closing the gap from ten seconds to four, but as the remaining laps entered single figures, he could make no more headway. Both drivers were credited with fastest lap, one minute 36.3 seconds—equal to Moss's pole time from the year before, with bigger engines.

Moss took the checkered flag just 3.6 seconds ahead, a remarkably close finish. Unpromising as the new 1.5-liter era of Formula 1 sounded, it had certainly gotten off to a dramatic start. But Moss would not be a player in it; such was Ferrari's dominance in 1961 that Moss took just one more championship race win, finishing third in the drivers' standings and had just reached a tentative deal to run a Ferrari in 1962 when a near-fatal accident in a non-championship race at Goodwood ended his top-line career.

HILL VS. STEWART VS. CLARK

From a purely superficial point of view, Graham Hill and Jackie Stewart had nothing in common, apart from the fact that they happened to be teammates when Stewart made his championship debut with British Racing Motors (BRM) in 1965. Hill, the son of a London stockbroker, had served in the navy, never even driven a car until the age of twenty-four, and had, in effect, talked his way into motorsports. He took a job at a racing school without much in the way of racing experience, and later, hitching a ride home from Brands Hatch with Lotus founder Colin Chapman in the mid-1950s, got a foot in the door as a mechanic. Hill epitomized the kind of driver whose success owed as much to focus, determination, and grit as it did to natural talent.

Stewart's father ran a car dealership, but Jackie suffered from dyslexia, and his electrifying gifts behind the wheel would come as a form of redemption after an unhappy time in the education system. He was ten years Hill's junior when he got his F1 break at the age of twenty-five. Even so, Hill, the 1962 world champion, clearly had a few years left in the tank. While Stewart

had perhaps more in common with his near-contemporary friend and fellow Scot Jim Clark, he watched and learned from Hill closely, absorbing the work ethic—but noting, too, how Hill's raffish charm and elegant sense of dress marked him out above other drivers.

Clark, hailing from a sheep-farming family from the Scottish borders, eschewed the public trappings of fame, even when he became wealthy. He was the favored son at Lotus, and the combination of his speed and finesse with Chapman's feverish creativity produced outright dominance—most of the time. It's no great exaggeration to say that Clark would either win a race or end up walking back to the pits because something had broken.

Clark and Hill dominated four of the five seasons of the 1.5-liter era, with Stewart joining the fray in the final one. Marginally better reliability enabled John Surtees to claim the title for Ferrari in 1964, but the agility of British-built cars would always be a deciding factor at Monaco. They had strength in numbers, too: if, say, Clark set pole in his Climax-engined Lotus but then retired from the race, as he did

in 1962 (clutch failure), 1963 (seized gearbox), and 1964 (engine failure), one or more of the other British "garagistes" would already be in the mix for the win.

In 1962, Hill snatched the lead at the start and led for most of the race until his new BRM V-8 engine failed with seven laps to go, enabling Bruce McLaren to inherit the lead in a Cooper-Climax and fend off Phil Hill's Ferrari by just over a second at the checkered flag. A year later, Hill and his BRM teammate Richie Ginther ran one-two in the early laps until Clark got by both of them, building a gradually increasing lead for fifty laps until his gearbox gave up, handing the initiative to Hill. In 1964, Clark led from the start until he had to pit so a loose suspension component could be bolted back into place, and he was charging back into contention when his engine failed with four laps to run. Hill won again, with a lap in hand above everyone else.

Clark's Indy 500 attempt meant he was absent from Monaco in 1965, and it was at this race where Hill earned his nickname, Mr. Monaco, recovering from adversity and facing down the challenge of Stewart, his new teammate, to claim a third consecutive Monaco victory. For a quarter of the race, this looked to be more or less a routine 1960s Monaco Grand Prix: Hill had set a pole time nearly four seconds faster

than the last one of the 2.5-liter era and roared off into an early lead ahead of Stewart, the Ferraris of John Surtees and Lorenzo Bandini, and Jack Brabham (now driving for his own eponymous team, with a Climax engine).

On lap twenty-five, Hill, unsighted by the downward slope of the road at the tunnel exit, narrowly missed a tangle with the tail-ender, Bob Anderson, and slid up the escape road at the chicane. Stewart, Bandini, Surtees, and Brabham all went by as Hill climbed out, pushed his car back onto the course, then got in again and tore off, now over thirty seconds in arrears.

"I was pretty narked [annoyed] about this," wrote Hill in his entry in the book *My Greatest Race*, in which he gives a highly illuminating description of the singular challenge of racing around Monaco. "It had more or less knocked me out of the fight for the lead. So I jumped into the car and set off in hot pursuit.

"Monte Carlo is an extremely difficult place to overtake anybody and you've really got to work at it. You start building up to pass somebody more or less a lap in advance. If you decide that the best place to take him is at the Gasworks corner, you've got to start the maneuver

more or less from the Gasworks on the preceding lap so that you arrive at Tabac—the one before the Gasworks—in just the right position to make a 100 percent job of taking the corner on the limit, and that little bit quicker, to draw alongside him going down the straight—and hoping to pass him under braking for the Gasworks corner.

"It takes a lot of planning, a lot of strategy, to actually pass somebody; it just doesn't occur in a flash if the bloke's going at roughly the same speed as you."

Stewart would go on to win the world title three times and is rightly remembered for his skill and precision. Here, though, in his second championship outing, he held the lead for just four laps before he spun at Sainte-Dévote and dropped to fourth place. Thus, Hill's first task as he raced back into contention was to pass his own teammate—who obligingly deferred to his senior, enabling Hill to set his sights on the two Ferraris up front. Bandini and Surtees were now fighting between themselves, having been passed by Brabham, whose engine then succumbed to an oil leak.

Ferrari team manager Eugenio Dragoni signaled his drivers to stop dicing with each other and to pick

their pace up, but Hill wasn't to be denied. First, he picked off Surtees, getting a better exit from Casino Square and annexing the inside line at Mirabeau, the right-hander roughly halfway down the hill where just a curb and a stone wall separated the road from a virtual cliff edge. Bandini defended stoutly, but Hill successfully replicated the move he'd made on Surtees and got his nose ahead into Mirabeau. Forty laps after losing the lead, Hill had it again—but there was still over a quarter of the race left to go, and Hill had to keep a resurgent Surtees at bay for a good twenty laps before the Ferraris fell away. Stewart finished third, one minute forty-one seconds down, after Surtees ran out of fuel on the penultimate lap.

"On the night of the race we went to the Tip Top," recorded Hill, "a little bar which doesn't seem to have much to recommend it except that it sells drink, but it is a popular meeting place for all the British contingent—we always go there.

"Every year the owner treats me to a drink—this time it was champagne."

In 1966, the engine formula changed again, to three-liter naturally aspirated form, and, as in 1961, the move caught many competitors unprepared. Brabham had planned well in advance and commissioned a bespoke Repco V-8 based on an Oldsmobile stock block, enabling his team to be dominant for two seasons. But not at Monaco in 1966: Stewart and Hill finished one-two using BRM V-8s stretched to a two-liter displacement, and might have repeated the feat in 1967 had that race not descended into chaos and catastrophe after Brabham's engine blew, depositing an oil slick; Bandini later suffered fatal burns in an accident at the chicane.

Hill moved to Lotus to be Clark's teammate in 1968 and bore the mantle of team leader following Clark's death in a Formula 2 accident. He would win the Monaco Grand Prix twice more before age and the results of a leg-breaking accident blunted his competitiveness, the last in 1969, when Stewart set pole but retired with a broken driveshaft. Stewart won the race twice more before retiring suddenly at the end of 1973, sad and angry at having lost so many friends to what he saw as needless accidents. That left the Monaco Grand Prix 5–3 in Hill's favor, with the peerless Clark—remarkably—on zero.

BRABHAM VS. RINDT

It's said that Jack Brabham saw something of himself in Jochen Rindt. Both were outwardly quiet and undemonstrative, but tigerish behind the wheel, and possessed of both a gift for mechanics and an entrepreneurial bent.

"We got on very well together," Brabham would later say. "And we had a lot of fun together as well. We used to have terrible dices on track, and we'd laugh about it all night."

It's unfortunate that Rindt moved from Cooper to Brabham's eponymous team in 1968, when the technical momentum of the three-liter formula had already shifted in favor of Ford's Cosworth-built DFV engine. Brabham's Repco engine was behind the development curve, and desperately so: adding multi-valve heads to liberate more power made it much less reliable. Rindt scored just two podium places and by the end of the season had confided to a friend, "I want to win the world championship so badly that I'm prepared to drive for Colin [Chapman] to do so." Chapman's Lotus cars, though fast and innovative, had a well-documented tendency to break, occasionally with fatal consequences.

Even so, Rindt duly went there in 1969, in a deal brokered by his manager, an entrepreneur who would go on to play a significant role in the growth of F1: Bernie Ecclestone. Chapman was to find Rindt an altogether different character from Jim Clark, the man he replaced. Clark was as diffident out of the car as he was transcendently quick within it. Rindt, though introverted, was opinionated and certainly not shy of expressing his thoughts.

Rindt's relationship with his new boss almost reached the breaking point at Monaco in 1969. This was an era in which designers had begun to garland cars with air foils at the front and rear to boost corner speeds; at the rear, these were usually mounted high, atop slim pillars. When Rindt's fell off at the Spanish Grand Prix—in the same place as teammate Graham Hill had lost his a few laps earlier—Rindt piled uncontrollably into the wreck of Hill's car, suffering a concussion, a broken nose, and a fractured jaw. From his hospital bed in Barcelona, he began to write letters, some to Chapman himself, others to motoring publications, declaiming the fragility of his car and the awfulness of wings.

The next round was at Monaco, and although Rindt was sitting it out while he recovered, his influence was felt. The Automobile Club de Monaco had no wish to see either the wings or a similar accident on their turf, but they had no power to outlaw the designs. Only the FIA's sporting committee could do that, so they convened a meeting on the first day of practice. By this point, Rindt and Chapman had ceased to be on speaking terms, communicating only via intermediaries, since Chapman was furious that his star driver's letter writing had in effect furnished the rule makers with the tools to peg Lotus back.

At the meeting, attended by only a handful of teams—Rob Walker would later claim that he learned of its outcome via a note slipped under his hotel door—the president of the sporting committee declared that high-mounted wings were to be banned immediately and the results of first practice were to be scratched. Fury ensued, but Lotus wasn't terminally inconvenienced; Hill took the last of his five Monaco Grand Prix victories by 17.3 seconds from Piers Courage in a privately entered Brabham. Digesting this result, Rindt confided in a friend, the journalist Heinz Prüller, "I am always in the wrong car at the wrong races at the wrong time."

It was only later in the season, as he considered his future, that Rindt reached a rapprochement with Chapman. He agreed to race with Chapman again in 1970, with the promise of a new car and the freedom to run an F2 team with his own name above the door, in partnership with Ecclestone.

The 1970 season began badly, as Lotus's radical new car, the 72, proved to be unreliable, fragile, and truculent. After failing to score in the opening two rounds, and suffering a scary accident in Spain, Rindt refused to race it in Monaco, where he qualified an aging 49C chassis eighth on the grid.

Quoted in David Tremayne's biography of Rindt, Ecclestone provides an illuminating anecdote that captures Rindt's mindset at this febrile time. In this era, drivers and personnel wore their credentials in the form of leather armbands; Rindt, on the grid, had his tucked into the pocket of his overalls, invisibly enough to attract the ire of an overly zealous policeman. "Here he [Rindt] is, in his racing suit, everybody knows who he is," says Ecclestone. "And the policeman started on him about his credential. So Jochen took the armband out of the front of his overalls and put it round his ankle.

"And when the policeman grabbed his leg and made as if to remove it, Jochen kicked him in the face. It was just before the start of the race, so we all hopped over to the car and just strong-armed the police out of the way."

Fourth on the grid, half way to pole, was Brabham. Now forty-four and already considering an offer from Ecclestone to buy his team, Brabham intended to leave F1 on a high note. The new BT33, the first Brabham to adopt monocoque chassis design, was competitive enough for him to have won the opening round in South Africa. But at Monaco he would have to outsmart the three drivers ahead of him first: Jackie Stewart (on pole, naturally) and Chris Amon in March cars built by Mosley and Herd's company, and his old teammate Denny Hulme in a McLaren. Separating him from eighth-placed Rindt were Jacky Ickx in a Ferrari and the Matras of Jean-Pierre Beltoise and Henri Pescarolo.

The race distance had been cut from one hundred laps to eighty in 1968, and for almost the first half of the grand prix, Rindt drove "like a taxi driver." Only on lap thirty-six did he pass Pescarolo, by which time Stewart had retired with engine failure, Brabham had passed Amon for the lead, and Ickx and Beltoise

had stopped because of transmission breakages.

So Rindt was now fourth, with some clear road ahead to Hulme. Galvanized now, Rindt caught Hulme and passed him just after half distance. Now Amon's team began to signal him that Rindt was thirteen seconds behind and closing. But Rindt wouldn't have to deal with the March on track: Amon's suspension broke on lap sixty-one. Now, with nineteen to go, victory was almost within sight. Or was it? The gap grew to fifteen seconds; perhaps, the pundits concluded, Rindt didn't have the appetite for it after all.

But as the laps remaining fell below single figures, Brabham was held up badly by tail-enders not once but twice. Once fifteen seconds ahead, now Brabham only had 4.4 seconds in hand over Rindt. Stewart had qualified in a time of one minute twenty-four seconds. Now, on the penultimate lap, Rindt punched in a one minute 23.2—the fastest of the race. He was but a second behind Brabham, and he continued to push over the final lap.

Rindt's cause seemed hopeless unless Brabham made a mistake, which surely he would not. But then, bearing down on the final corner, Brabham exceeded even his prodigious mental bandwidth: he lapped Piers Courage and was about to lap Hulme, all the

while monitoring his mirrors for the red and gold Lotus, when he braked just fractions of a second too late and skittered wide, into the barrier. Rindt was so *on it*—his last lap was recorded as one minute 23.2 seconds, fastest once again—that he initially failed to register that he'd won the race.

Rindt had not only beaten his old boss, he'd forced him into a humiliating error. Brabham would call time on his career at season's end.

Rindt never got to race at Monaco again. A mechanical failure pitched him into the barriers at Monza at high speed during qualifying for the Italian Grand Prix in early autumn. Rindt, who declined to wear a full racing harness because he found the crotch straps uncomfortable, suffered fatal injuries. He remains F1's posthumously crowned champion.

"WITH TEARS ROLLING DOWN HIS FACE, JOCHEN LOOKED LIKE A MAN COMING OUT OF A TRANCE . . ."

—NIGEL ROEBUCK ON THE 1970 MONACO GRAND PRIX

SENNA VS. PROST

Just two names appear on the roster of winners for ten consecutive Monaco Grands Prix between 1984 and 1993: Ayrton Senna and Alain Prost. Not only were these the greatest drivers of overlapping generations, they represented a fascinating contrast of styles—and, deliciously, spent two seasons as implacably opposed teammates. All Formula 1 fans have an opinion on which was the best driver, and yet if you look to Monaco—surely a rigorous barometer of driver ability—to provide a definitive guide, you will not find the answer in the results sheets alone.

The score is six-four to Senna, and yet for four of the races, Senna was in markedly inferior equipment. In the two where they shared equal equipment, each won a race. And to add a note of rigor, we must factor in that Prost was absent for Senna's victory in 1992, sitting out the season in an enforced sabbatical after falling out with Ferrari during the 1991 season.

Senna's advocates point first to the 1984 race, which was halted—partly at Prost's insistence—after just thirty-one laps, owing to a heavy downpour. Prost collected the win, but it was a Pyrrhic victory—only half the points were awarded, and, at the end of the season, he lost the championship to his McLaren teammate Niki Lauda by half a point. Who knows what would have happened if that year's Monaco Grand Prix had been allowed to go the distance? Senna, in his debut season and driving an unfancied Toleman car, used the foul conditions as a calling card and was reeling Prost in as the laps ticked by. But he had also damaged a suspension wishbone by striking a curb too heavily. Had the race actually gone on, he might have had to retire; Prost might have won anyway. It is one of F1's imponderables.

Senna moved to the more competitive Lotus-Renault team in 1985 and qualified on pole, but then retired from the lead when his engine failed. Prost swept in through the open door and was unchallenged after Michele Alboreto's Ferrari suffered a puncture. McLaren continued to be the dominant force throughout the 1986 season, when Prost won a processional Monaco Grand Prix from pole position with Senna in third.

By 1987, McLaren's TAG-Porsche engine was no longer the most

powerful. Senna's Lotus team had prudently moved to Honda power, and while the Lotus chassis wasn't a match for Williams, the other Honda-equipped team, Senna's brilliance told at Monaco: Nigel Mansell qualified on pole for Williams with Senna alongside, and when Mansell's engine lost boost pressure, Senna went by for what would prove to be the easiest of his Monaco victories. Prost halted with engine failure four laps from the end.

The years 1988 and 1989, when Senna and Prost were paired at McLaren with Honda power, were the most intriguing. Senna's 1988 qualifying lap has rightly been enshrined in legend for his 1.427-second advantage over Prost is inarguable. And yet he made a mistake in the race and crashed out at Portier with twelve laps to go. Famously, he was so disgusted with himself that he walked straight home to his apartment.

The following year, his turbulent relationship with Prost now entering its terminally dysfunctional phase, Senna outqualified his teammate by the slightly more modest margin of 1.148 seconds. After seventy-seven uneventful laps, Senna crossed the line 52.529 seconds ahead of his teammate. Third-placed Stefano Modena was a lap down. It was one of those days, prevalent during 1988 and 1989, when anyone not in a McLaren must have wondered why they had bothered turning up.

From 1989 until 1993, at five consecutive Monaco Grands Prix, Senna was the winner. To say that Prost had no answer would be unfair, since in 1990 he was running second when his electrics failed, and in 1991 he had to make an extra pit stop for a loose wheel nut to be tightened. But in both those races, Senna was already ahead.

In 1993, the last time they would encounter one another in Monaco, the situation was thrillingly poised: Prost had the all-conquering Renault-engined Williams FW14C at his disposal, while Senna was grudgingly agreeing his services with McLaren on a race-by-race basis, so woeful did he feel their situation was with a customer Ford engine. But on the streets of Monaco, Prost's power advantage would surely be neutralized.

That's not quite how it panned out in qualifying, since Senna had injured himself in a practice crash and could do no better than third on the grid. Still, Prost contrived to jump the start from pole position, earning himself a ten-second stop-go penalty, and then he stalled his car after serving it. Michael Schumacher led until his hydraulic system failed,

handing the race to Senna—who cruised home with a comfortable margin over Prost's teammate Damon Hill, while Prost was classified fourth, a lap down.

The argument over whether Senna was a better driver than Prost is one for the ages. What's most extraordinary is that these bitter rivals, who clashed so many times on track, rarely came close to disputing the same patch of real estate on the streets of Monaco.

"YOUR IDEAL TEAMMATE IS ANYONE THREE SECONDS A LAP SLOWER—THAT'S WHY SENNA WAS HAPPIER WITH ME AT MCLAREN THAN HE WAS WITH PROST."
—GERHARD BERGER

MANSELL VS. SENNA

Such was Nigel Mansell's car advantage during 1992 that he had the world championship in the bag by mid-season. And Mansell, who had undergone considerable suffering and adversity throughout his racing career—from breaking his neck in Formula 3 to having a (Lotus) team boss who said, "Nigel Mansell will never win a grand prix so long as I have a hole in my arse"—often seemed among those most frustrated by his Williams-Renault's superiority. After so many years of being defined by underdog toil, having the best car sat rather ill.

Monaco 1992 put that into perspective for him.

Mansell and Senna had been alongside each other on the front row at Monaco in 1987. Now Mansell was starting ahead of Senna for the first time since then. And, as in 1987, car trouble would play a part in the outcome.

After five consecutive wins, Mansell was already virtually untouchable in the drivers' standings. His teammate, the veteran Riccardo Patrese—Monaco winner in 1982— had pushed him closely for much of the preceding season, but the addition of active suspension to the

Williams FW14B put daylight between them. At the limits of tire adhesion, the active suspension transmitted very little feel to the driver; pushing it to the edge was an act of sheer bravery and faith that Mansell could summon, but Patrese could not.

From the start, Mansell simply drove away from the field as Senna burst forward from third on the grid to usurp Patrese for second place. But Senna could do nothing about Mansell. The gap just grew and grew. Mansell was determined to win Monaco for the first time in his career.

On lap seventy-one, just seven from the checkered flag, and with thirty

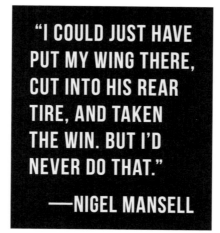

"I COULD JUST HAVE PUT MY WING THERE, CUT INTO HIS REAR TIRE, AND TAKEN THE WIN. BUT I'D NEVER DO THAT."

—NIGEL MANSELL

seconds in hand over Senna, Mansell corrected a brief but savage rear-end slide at Portier. At first glance, it looked like driver error. Mansell thought he had a puncture. The post-race inquiry determined that a wheel nut had come loose.

As Mansell crawled back to the pits, his lead evaporated. When the Williams rejoined, Senna was over five seconds ahead, and Mansell demolished the gap. For the final three laps he was all over Senna's gearbox, feinting and jinking from one side to the other at every corner, but even on fresh tires there was no way past. Mansell balked at the notion of "giving him a nudge," and Senna was never going to leave him the slightest gap to use as a foothold, so they finished nose to tail—the closest Monaco finish ever. It was a thrilling end to what had been an unpromising race.

OLIVIER'S DAY IN THE SUN

There have been several lucky winners of the Monaco Grand Prix, but no undeserving ones.

Fourteenth on the grid for the 1996 Monaco Grand Prix was a promising twenty-nine-year-old Frenchman, Olivier Panis. His Ligier team had been acquired by Benetton bosses Flavio Briatore and Tom Walkinshaw the previous season, principally in order to transfer the Renault engine supply to Benetton. Ligier thus became a satellite operation, running visually similar cars built around identical monocoques, but powered by bought-in Mugen-Honda engines.

Panis's grid spot was therefore disappointingly unrepresentative. He'd ended 1995 with a podium finish in Australia, on the streets of Adelaide, and bagged three points in the early races of 1996. In Monaco, though, his JS43 developed a misfire whose cause eluded both the Ligier mechanics and the Mugen engineers. Stumped, they stripped the car and prepared for an all-nighter ahead of race day. Panis skipped dinner and hung around the garage, searching for words of encouragement.

"I went round the mechanics and said, 'We can still finish on the podium,'" he recalls. "I saw the looks from them that said, 'This guy is nice, but he's fucking crazy.'"

The year 1996 had begun with Williams-Renault dominant after two seasons of being shown the way by Michael Schumacher and Benetton—from whom Schumacher had taken his leave, transferring his allegiance to Ferrari. Damon Hill had established himself as the Williams team leader in the wake of Ayrton Senna's tragic death a season and a half earlier, much as his father had stabilized Lotus after Jim Clark's fatal accident in 1968. And yet, even in his world championship year, the underrated Hill would not be able to join his father on the list of Monaco winners.

Ferrari was only at the beginning of a competitive upswing after years in the doldrums, but, around Monaco, Schumacher's genius outweighed any deficiencies in horsepower or handling. He had already nailed three podium finishes in the ungainly F310, and here he claimed pole position ahead of Hill. The Benettons

of Jean Alesi and Gerhard Berger lined up behind. The weekend was unfolding as expected. Nobody could have predicted what would happen next.

Panis arrived at the Ligier garage—like all the others, a temporary facility off the Boulevard Albert I—for the pre-race warmup session to discover a far more buoyant mood prevailing. His car was ready, and fixed. Panis went out and set the fastest lap of the session. Traditionally, the warmup was a strong signifier of race pace, but since Panis was only fourteenth on the grid—in Monaco—few people paid great heed. Surely, he was starting too far back to make an impact.

But already the rain clouds were rolling in.

When the rain arrived, it did so in such volume that the organizers felt it prudent to arrange an additional session so that the drivers could acclimatize to the conditions. Several, including McLaren's Mika Häkkinen, crashed, and the chaos continued when the race began, even though the rain had abated.

Just as his father had hoodwinked Jim Clark twice back in the 1960s, Hill made a crisp getaway from second on the grid to sweep past

Schumacher on the first lap. Three cars crashed at the first corner, and Schumacher himself, an acknowledged master in slippery conditions, spun off before the first lap was over.

As the casualty list mounted, Hill built an ever-increasing lead and Panis bided his time, feeling his way through the conditions. But Panis wasn't shy of taking a few risks, passing first Martin Brundle's Jordan, then Häkkinen. This, plus attrition as others fell by the wayside, left him in eighth place as the race closed in on half distance. That podium didn't seem so unlikely now.

As the track began to dry and the wet-weather tires wore out, the key challenge for the drivers was to identify the crossover point where it became advantageous to pit for the "slick" dry-weather tires. For the first one to make the call, it is a moment of extreme, but calculated, risk. Panis asked his team to watch for the first driver to pit for slicks and to report on his progress.

That man was Hill, and he was instantly quick on the new rubber. Panis followed suit. Many of the others were too slow on the uptake. Wary of straying too far from the dry line but feeling the grip build, Panis made a move on Eddie Irvine, Schumacher's teammate, at the Loews hairpin, nudging him off in the process. Now he was third, behind Hill and Alesi, and had that podium finish in his hands.

Then, more drama: on the fortieth lap, Hill's engine blew. Twenty laps later, Alesi's suspension gave way, and Panis was in the lead. But now, like any gambler, he had to hold his nerve: the slow pace of those early laps meant the race would be flagged at the two-hour cut-off point before reaching the planned seventy-eight laps, but Panis was low on fuel. On the Ligier pit wall, the engineers reluctantly concluded that he would have to make a splash-and-dash pit stop, and signaled him to do so.

Panis ignored them. Even as Häkkinen's McLaren teammate David Coulthard closed in, Panis calmly short-shifted through the gears, lifted off early for the corners, and turned a deaf ear to his engineer's increasingly shrill radio calls. As Panis went past the pit entry for the penultimate time, they were still begging him to stop. The final lap, he concedes, felt like it lasted an age. By now, just four cars were running on the track.

Panis, through judgement, skill, and sheer bravery, had ensured he was at the head of them.

YOU CAN'T PARK THERE

"Do you feel that you cheated, Michael?"

The question—posed by *Daily Mirror* journalist Byron Young—went off like an incendiary device in the charged atmosphere of the post-qualifying press conference. Who dares speak to a seven-time world champion like that? No wonder Michael Schumacher's face contorted into a grotesque rictus of disgruntlement.

Nevertheless, he was caught red-handed.

Schumacher remains the most successful grand prix driver of all time—and, but for a few Clark-like moments of misfortune, could have won more Monaco grands prix than anyone else. But he is also a divisive figure, tainted by allegations not only that he was complicit in cheating—that he won races in cars believed to be illegal—but also that on several occasions, he overstepped the mark of what is permissible conduct on track.

The technical complaints are unsubstantiated, but there is no denying that Schumacher could be heavy-handed in the heat of the moment. Twice he took out rivals during title-deciding grands prix: in 1994, he sealed the championship in his favor by sideswiping Damon Hill in Adelaide; in 1997, he performed a similar maneuver on Jacques Villeneuve at Jerez, this time failing to come home with the silverware.

For several years thereafter, his driving remained forceful at times, but once Ferrari attained technical superiority in the early 2000s, Schumacher generally controlled races from the front, winning five consecutive world titles. It was only at the end of his reign that he found himself on the back foot once again.

New rules for 2005—mandating, among other things, no tire stops except in case of emergency—temporarily brought a halt to Schumacher's and Ferrari's dominance and enabled Renault prodigy Fernando Alonso to win the world championship. And, although the no-stops rule was repealed for 2006, Renault's Michelin tires usually had the edge on Ferrari's Bridgestones, handing Alonso an advantage once again.

So, when Schumacher set provisional pole at Monaco as the final seconds of the qualifying session

ticked by, it looked like a fascinating contest was in prospect, for Alonso was about to embark on his own hot lap. But then Schumacher locked a wheel at La Rascasse, the final corner, and came to rest with his Ferrari's nose against the barrier. Out came the yellow flags and Alonso had to abort his hot lap.

Schumacher initially claimed that it was an accident and that he had simply been trying too hard to improve his time. Nobody bought this argument. Schumacher's rivals, and other team bosses, eagerly decanted their thoughts into reporters' microphones. The stewards convened, examined the evidence, and stripped him of pole position. He would start the race from the back of the grid.

"Rascasse-gate" is still a defining moment of Schumacher's career, in part because of the brazen nature of the act, but also the rather crass way he and his entourage tried to ride out the controversy. For many years, he simply refused to talk about it.

"Do you feel that you cheated, Michael?"

"Whatever you do in certain moments," said Schumacher, "your enemies believe one thing and the people who support you believe another."

FROM THE ASHES OF DISASTER

A skilled gambler calculates hundreds of probabilities without twitching an eyebrow. F1 teams have rooms full of mathematicians, operating simulation software, to crunch more potential outcomes than there are stars in the sky.

These processes take place behind closed doors, back at team headquarters. As each race progresses, the backroom strategists monitor every car on track, narrowing down the number of possible outcomes. Sometimes they make a call early on that proves inspired.

Seldom has that been more apparent than at Monaco in 2008. A rain squall before the start threw all the chips in the air. McLaren's Lewis Hamilton, championship runner-up the previous season, was running second to the Ferrari of Felipe Massa when he entered Tabac just a little too hot on the sixth lap, tapping the barrier at the exit. Almost instantly, his tire deflated.

There are hundreds of sensors on an F1 car. The strategists in "Mission Control" back at McLaren's base saw the problem immediately and began to calculate all the possible scenarios.

Tabac is but a few hundred meters from the pit entry. It was perhaps twenty-five to thirty seconds before Hamilton would arrive in his pit box—barely time to get a new set of tires ready.

Before those seconds had elapsed, "Mission Control" had drilled through the potential outcomes. With rain still falling, should he take on the "extreme" wet tires, which offered better water dispersal at the cost of short life when the track dried, or the more risky intermediate option? They chose the latter. The next choice was how much fuel to add, and this would dictate the length of the stop. Looking at where the other cars were on track, McLaren's strategists felt they could add enough fuel for Hamilton to complete the whole race and still get him out in fifth place, ahead of a train of cars being held up by the Toyota of Jarno Trulli.

McLaren's pit crew executed the stop perfectly. His cause aided by a safety car period shortly afterwards, Hamilton took the lead when his rivals pitted, then benefitted from a short stop for dry-weather tires.

From the outside, this victory looked seamless, if a little fortuitous—but it was dictated by a handful of smart minds working in unison, and with but a handful of seconds to calculate the odds.

STARS AND CARS

THE FAIRY-TALE PRINCESS

"Some stone—did you mine it yourself?" Bing Crosby's ad lib to Grace Kelly in her final film, the 1956 musical comedy *High Society*, aptly captures the scale of the 10.47-carat diamond in the center of her Cartier engagement ring.

There is a certain circularity to Grace Kelly's transition from movie star to fairy-tale princess, spritzing Monaco's soiled postwar reputation and presiding over the principality's rebirth as a favorable destination for the international jet set. She starred opposite Cary Grant in *To Catch a Thief*, a crime caper set in the French Riviera milieu, concerning a former jewel thief's efforts to establish his innocence. It was while doing publicity for this movie that she met Prince Rainier of Monaco at the 1955 Cannes Film Festival. Having played a princess on screen, she would become one for real.

Kelly's career as an actress shone as briefly and brightly as a shooting star. Born in Philadelphia in 1929 and hailing from wealthy stock, she moved to New York shortly after leaving high school and worked her way into acting, making her Broadway debut at the age of nineteen.

"In 1947," wrote the critic Anthony Lane in a 2010 *New Yorker* piece,

"before enrolling at the American Academy of Dramatic Arts, which charged a cool five hundred dollars a year, she moved to New York, where she resided, as nice young ladies did, at the Barbizon Hotel for Women, at Lexington and Sixty-Third Street, and had an affair with an actor and director eleven years her senior, as nice young ladies didn't."

From there, she took on minor roles in the emergent medium of television drama before chasing the acting dream westward to California. She got her big-screen break in the 1951 noir thriller *14 Hours* and achieved wider notice in the 1952 Gary Cooper western *High Noon*, but it wasn't until 1954 that she would achieve stardom. Then, in short order, she shared top billing with James Stewart in the Alfred Hitchcock thriller *Rear Window* and won the Best Actress Oscar for her part in the now largely forgotten drama *The Country Girl*. Two years later, *High Society* marked her retirement from the big screen at the age of twenty-six.

The courtship between Kelly and Rainier was equally brief and to the point. After her return to the United States, they corresponded, and later in 1955, Rainier flew over to meet her (staunchly Catholic) family and

propose in person. Just two hurdles remained, one far less public than the other: a fertility test and the question of a dowry.

In 1955, Rainier was a man under pressure, both financially and from the onward march of the biological clock. Monaco's exchequer remained in a critical state, and while Rainier was supposedly one of the world's most eligible bachelors, at the age of thirty-two, he was running short on time to meet a suitable partner and begin the constitutionally necessary process of producing heirs. He'd lived with the actress Gisèle Pascal in a villa on Saint-Jean-Cap-Ferrat for six years, only for her supposed infertility to nix the romance. Kelly—world-famous, attractive, most probably fertile—would tick the requisite boxes in terms of forming a glamorous power couple to head Monaco's renaissance and secure the Grimaldi dynasty.

The fertility test was the subject of a discreet proposal and careful secrecy, and was performed by Rainier's personal physician in a private clinic outside Philadelphia. What Grace's father, the construction magnate Jack Kelly, made of the demand for a $2 million dowry is a matter of speculation, but he paid in full and maximized the publicity he gained from the engagement.

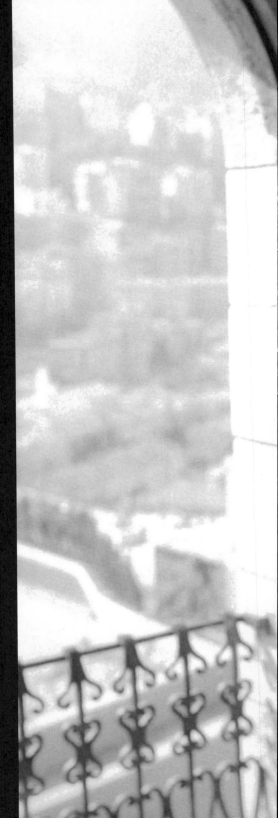

This was December 1955. On April 4, 1956, Kelly boarded the SS *Constitution* in New York, ready to begin her new life. There were two separate wedding ceremonies—one civil, one religious—with a lobster banquet and a seven-month honeymoon cruise to follow. From then until her death, Grace was an regular fixture at the Monaco Grand Prix, touring the course beforehand with her husband in an open-top car and appearing in the podium afterwards with the winning drivers.

The union produced three children, Princesses Caroline and Stéphanie, and Prince Albert. But was it a happy one? Princess Grace has been the subject of innumerable biographies and scandal-raking stories, and, of course, a TV movie starring Cheryl Ladd. It's claimed that the marriage only came about through the influence of Aristotle Onassis, with whom Rainier was wrestling for practical control of Monaco's engines of wealth. Claims also abound of infidelity on both sides—and that the stifling environment of Monaco was deleterious to Kelly's mental health. One book claims that she began to consider herself "a prisoner in a golden cage." Certainly, she suffered bouts of depression and was known to drink heavily on occasion.

On the afternoon of September 13, 1982, she declined the services of a chauffeur to carry her and Princess Stéphanie from their home on Mont Agel down to Monaco. Rainier, it's said, disapproved of her driving. As they made their way down the steep and winding Route de La Turbie, the car ploughed straight on at a hairpin bend and plunged down the mountainside. Princess Stéphanie suffered a hairline fracture to a vertebra, from which she would eventually recover; Princess Grace's injuries were more severe—and terminal. She was taken off life support the next day.

The circumstances of her death are the subject of speculation as fevered as that about her life. Officially, she suffered a stroke and lost consciousness at the wheel. Alternative narratives thrown up over the years have placed Stéphanie at the wheel and Grace under the influence of anything from alcohol to prescription drugs. The truth is enshrouded in layers of myth—the most pernicious of which is, no doubt, the ever-present Curse of the Grimaldis. In death as in life, Princess Grace remains an object of fascination.

MASTERS OF MONACO

The Monaco Grand Prix exerts an irresistible pull on racing fanatics and fame junkies alike. Celebrities arrive to see and be seen; in 2018 alone, one could walk through the paddock and stumble upon the likes of Hugh Grant, George Lucas, sundry supermodels, and members of the cast of *Game of Thrones*. Racing teams engage in their own off-track competitions to invite the hottest guests. Outside the paddock, paparazzi and selfie stick–wielding members of the public jostle for a view of the denizens within.

But celebrity ebbs and flows. The names and faces have changed over the years. So have the racing cars. But one thing has altered only by degree since 1929: the physical and mental challenges of racing at round the streets of Monaco. In the past, it has broken the weak, the unfortunate, and the merely quite good. Even the likes of Nelson Piquet, a three-time world champion who described the grand prix as "like racing a bicycle around your living room," never won here.

There is no experience on earth equivalent to watching a track session at Monaco from just beyond the barriers—which, given the right

ticket or a media tabard, you can do. From the media center and paddock area, you can track the outside of the course, walking the narrow harborside vestibule between the water and the Armco barrier, past the bust of Louis Chiron and on to Tabac. Here you can experience the sheer violence of the passage of an F1 car at full chat as it skims the barrier almost within touching distance. The very air feels as if it's being bullied out of the way.

Keep on moving. To the left, the barriers, the legs chocked into place with wooden wedges. To the right, a phalanx of expensive yachts in which the privileged few sip cocktails and absorb the sun and spectacle. Note how one is called Gatsby, the owner surely missing the point of Fitzgerald's novel. At the chicane, where the photographers lie face down to capture dramatic angles of the cars slip-sliding through the left-right-right-left, note how some drivers hook the right-rear wheel over the "sausage curb" on the inside, the better to rotate the car quickly. It's happening just meters away.

When the marshal nods to tell you it's clear, you can edge behind the stone balustrade leading to the yacht club and enjoy the ear-splitting delights of the tunnel. Then it's up to you: walk on, out of the tunnel, to Portier, or duck and dive through the system of elevators in the bowels of the hotel and casino to stand by the rows of Bird of Paradise flowers behind the barrier at Massenet, where you can watch the cars roar up the hill and around into Casino Square. It should be an utterly alien environment for a racing car.

Monaco, wrote Graham Hill in the book *My Greatest Race*, "is always a tricky race, one of the trickiest circuits in the world, because it is so easy to be just a little bit untidy at any one particular corner, clobber a curb with the wheel and break the suspension or break a wheel or cause yourself to spin off. And, of course, there is just nowhere to spin at Monte Carlo; you bounce off hotels, nightclubs, brick walls, telegraph poles, and street lamps. Everything around is absolutely solid, although we have managed to get a few Armco barriers set up at one or two spots which might prevent us from coming to a stop rather smartly."

Since Hill set down those words, most—but not all—of the hazards have been shuffled behind the Armco, but these streets retain a threat. They're narrow. There are manhole covers (in 2010, the Brazilian driver

Rubens Barrichello crashed when one of his wheels spat a loose manhole cover into his car). There are oil remnants dropped by buses and trucks.

"The driving challenge is off the scale," says David Coulthard, twice a winner here. "Your senses are attacked. Everything is louder. It's all about precision, threading a needle at very high speed . . . you have to know every inch of the track, in the same way you would know your way around your own house if the electricity went off and you were plunged into sudden darkness. To win here is the most rewarding thing a grand prix driver can do."

Given the scale of the challenge, it's little wonder that the list of serial Monaco Grand Prix winners reads like a roster of the all-time greats. Juan Manuel Fangio, Stirling Moss, Graham Hill, Jackie Stewart, Niki Lauda, Alain Prost, Ayrton Senna, Michael Schumacher . . . and there are some surprising omissions, such as Jim Clark. The Monaco Grand Prix can be every bit as cruel as the Indy 500 or the Le Mans 24 Hours.

As Daniel Ricciardo—who bears all the hallmarks of becoming a modern master of Monaco—said after he was robbed of victory by a botched pit stop in 2016, "How do I feel? Like I've been run over by an eighteen-wheel truck."

CONQUERING THE SEA

Circumnavigate the Rock by path and escalator, if you're on foot, or by tunnel if you're in a car, and you'll find yourself in the entirely modern suburb of Fontvieille. Here you'll find the Columbus Hotel, once co-owned by double Monaco Grand Prix winner David Coulthard; the pleasingly diverting Museum of Stamps and Coins; the Stade Louis II, home of the soccer club AS Monaco; the Princess Grace Rose Garden; a yacht harbor; the Monaco Top Cars Collection, home to Prince Rainier's car collection, including the 1929 Monaco Grand Prix–winning car, plus a number of later additions; a heliport connecting Monaco with the Nice airport; and an architecturally homogenous array of shopping centers and apartment blocks.

It's modern and homogenous simply because it didn't exist until the 1970s. Before Prince Rainier embarked on a huge expansion of Monaco in the 1960s, this area belonged to the Mediterranean Sea.

Fontvieille and the Larvotto district, which lies to the east and includes artificial beaches, the Grimaldi Forum conference center, and the Monte Carlo Sporting Club, addressed a problem that crept up on Monaco as its population and prosperity grew under Rainier. Real estate quickly began to run short. The Monaco skyline you see today—modern high-rises clustered on the hill like barnacles in place of the Belle Époque villas of the nineteenth century—offered only a partial solution.

By 1960, people and money were flooding in to Monaco as Rainier's glitzy showbiz marriage rinsed the principality's grubby reputation and put it on the US investment map; it benefitted, too, from ongoing austerity measures elsewhere in Europe, as recovering countries sought to rebuild their depleted exchequers (and pay off US war debts) through tax. The elites of Europe alighted upon Monaco again as a means of sheltering their wealth from the prying eyes of the taxman. Rainier discovered a love of building, much as his wife pushed back against the destruction of classical features to make way for new developments. The tug of war between the two is reflected in the inconsistency of the built environment around the heart of Monaco: the Hermitage, the casino, a number of Belle Époque buildings, and the

venerable stone balustrades around the harbor escaped the bulldozers, but modern edifices were shoehorned in and around them. Some, such as the Loews Hotel (now the Fairmont), were practically chiseled into the stone itself; the construction of Loews tripled the length of the tunnel through which the Monaco Grand Prix circuit passes.

Rainier achieved all this, and a revolution in the Monégasque economy, in the teeth of opposition from two very powerful but very different men: Aristotle Onassis and Charles de Gaulle. Onassis had performed an under-the-radar acquisition of SBM, the monopoly casino and hotel operator, during the 1950s, and, while this had shored up the Grimaldi regime's perilous cash position (since a generous portion of the receipts flowed in to the family coffers), it also made Onassis a powerful voice. Because his vision of Monaco's future differed enormously from Rainier's—Onassis wanted to enshrine Monaco as, in effect, a gated community for the wealthy elite, while Rainier sought to broaden and diversify its economy to generate new revenue streams— conflict was inevitable.

But not before Rainier had to see off an equally single-minded and intransigent figure from across the border. Charles de Gaulle was a giant of postwar French politics, a decorated soldier who had seen service in both world wars and become a figurehead of the French resistance against Nazi Germany. In both that and his postwar career in government, he was often as vehemently opposed to his allies as he was to his enemies. As president of France in the early 1960s, he began to chafe against the flow of French nationals taking up residence in Monaco, and, being fond of grand-gesture politics, in 1962 he made his feelings known by blockading the roads to the principality.

Compared with the contemporaneous Cuban missile crisis, it was the proverbial storm in a teacup, but the blockade stood for six months. Rainier had to pacify De Gaulle by removing tax privileges from French citizens and redrawing Monaco's constitution to include a French minister of state.

Now temporarily relieved of one thorn in his side, Rainier could deal with Onassis, which he did with a breathtaking piece of subterfuge in 1964: massively diluting Onassis's shareholding in SBM overnight by issuing 600,000 shares, which the state bought at a fraction of their face value. Shortly afterwards, Onassis literally sailed off into the sunset on his yacht, *Christina*.

With Monaco's principal economic engine now under his control, Rainier could press ahead largely unopposed. France pushed back against his land reclamation projects, though not enough to string up barbed wire at the border again, and the matter of air and sea rights was eventually resolved amicably between Rainier and one of De Gaulle's successors, François Mitterrand, in 1984.

In the twenty-first century, income from the casino now represents a small percentage of the state's take. Tourism, other light industries, and receipts from value-added tax (ironically, a much more regressive form of taxation than income tax) account for the majority of earnings. And the concrete is still being poured: at the outside of the grand prix circuit's Portier bend, a $1.2 billion six-hectare lump of prime real estate is being annexed from the sea. It will accommodate new luxury apartments, mansions—and, yes, casinos.

CIRCUIT EVOLUTION

You don't come to the Monaco Grand Prix to watch an event packed with overtaking maneuvers—because if you do, you'll be disappointed. The nature of the environment militates against easy passing; such overtaking as you do see will arise through either careful planning or opportunism, bravery, and enforced capitulation. As such, it will be diamond grade.

After finishing third in a largely processional 2018 Monaco Grand Prix, no less an eminence than Lewis Hamilton, one of the greats of his generation, called for a change of format to maintain the event's status as one of Formula 1's crown jewels. During a rambling and somewhat peculiar post-race soliloquy in his Mercedes team's motor home, Hamilton suggested that, among other measures, the circuit's layout could be revised to include different streets.

Some cried that this was sacrilege; others pointed out that Anthony Noghès thought that his original layout was the only one possible, and that little had changed in the interim to disprove his conviction. But the layout and furniture of the Monaco Grand Prix *has* changed in many ways since 1929, in some ways more than others.

The quayside supporting the steel-and-glass edifice from where Hamilton delivered his speech didn't exist back then. Even today, it isn't quite large enough to support the spatial requirements of the contemporary mine's-bigger-than-yours F1 paddock: the Red Bull motor home sits outside the paddock, floating in the harbor. Small-scale land reclamation since the 1990s has created space around the swimming pool for modern safety requirements and for the pit lane and garages to become permanent structures. Until comparatively recently, entrants had to work on their cars in the side streets; later, in a multistory car park. Today the supporting events—the Porsche Supercup, GP3, and Formula 2—still have to work in the car park.

In most other respects, the circuit is a fascinating time capsule—just 157 meters longer now than it was in 1929. Around it, the cityscape has changed almost beyond recognition, but for the stone balustrades and fragments of throwback architecture, such as the Hermitage and the casino. The high-grip asphalt of the track surface itself has nothing in common with the dusty, rutted roads of the 1920s, crisscrossed by streetcar lines.

Until 1950, and then again from 1972 until the present day, the start line has been on what is now called Boulevard Albert I. From here, it's a short blast of acceleration until the track turns sharply right and heads uphill at the Place Sainte Dévote, a junction named after Monaco's patron saint. Developments here in 1976 made the corner slightly tighter, and the pit exit was relocated here in 2003. You'll also find a life-size bronze statue of Juan-Manuel Fangio and his Mercedes W154 here.

The uphill stretch towards Massenet and Casino Square is as it was, though the names on the designer shops that front it have changed many times, and Armco barriers now separate the fans and track workers from the action. Armco also militates against cars coming to grief as the track plunges back downhill after Mirabeau and towards what was once the station hairpin. In the 1950s, train drivers would regularly come to an unscheduled halt on the viaduct spanning this crevasse to get a better view of the track action, but the station was relocated to make way for the Loews Hotel

development in 1973, which also more than tripled the length of the tunnel the track passes through as it returns along the waterside.

Monaco's sharp, rocky topography dictates an almost straight line from the tunnel exit to where Tabac marks the corner of the harbor. From the earliest days, it was obvious that something had to be done to reduce the speeds at which cars arrive at Tabac, as any mistake there would send cars clattering into the stone steps or through the window of the eponymous shop itself. A chicane of some sort has been a permanent but never quite satisfactory feature in this area; its location and severity has been changed many times, particularly in response to Lorenzo Bandini's death in 1967. It remains a shock to the system as drivers emerge into daylight from the tunnel, the downward slope of the road hindering visibility and acting against the effectiveness of the brakes.

Tabac has also been sharpened through an extension to the harborside. In the 1950s, the best and most spectacular drivers would wriggle through this fast left-hander in a four-wheel drift; the advent of wings and better tire technology has rendered this element of sensing the queasy equilibrium between grip

and breakaway redundant. Now, it's a lift and a downshift—the aerodynamic loadings in a modern F1 car are such that simply doing this is equivalent to you standing on the brakes of your road car hard enough to lock the wheels.

Post-Tabac, the circuit ran straight until the Gasworks hairpin, where it looped back onto the Boulevard Albert I. Between 1955 and 1972, this was also the start-finish straight, overlooked by a massive and rickety-looking grandstand. The removal of the gasometer and the erection of the swimming pool changed the complexion of this last section of the lap; there are now two chicanes in rapid succession as the track jinks around the pool, then goes left-right-right-right around La Rascasse, a famous and popular nightspot, if one that doesn't quite justify its bar prices. It's here that Ivan Capelli made an unusual blunder in 1993, spinning his Ferrari and coming to rest with one rear wheel atop the barrier.

The final corner, just after the new pit entry, was named in honor of the race's founder: Anthony Noghès. Quite what he would have made of this tight right-hander is a matter of speculation.

SAFETY FAST

That accidents during the Monaco Grand Prix are seldom injurious is a testament to the skill of modern drivers, the quality of car engineering, and the vigilance of the organizers and racing's governing body.

At the time of writing, the lap record is held by Max Verstappen at one minute 14.26 seconds, an average speed of 100.52 miles per hour. Rudolf Caracciola set the prewar lap record of one minute 46.5 seconds, an average of 66.79 miles per hour, in 1937. Amendments to the track have rendered this comparison not entirely rigorous, but the fact remains that the Monaco Grand Prix is now faster and more demanding than ever before.

While a good many of the safety improvements have come from lessons learned through catastrophes elsewhere, such as having Armco barriers lining the track, specific incidents at Monaco have informed developments here. Sainte Dévote, as the first corner, is a natural scene for collisions, such as when Derek Daly went airborne at the start of the race in 1980. Widening the road at the entry here and providing more runoff area—and lining that with tire walls

and Tecpro barriers—has lessened the consequences of accidents. But mitigating the consequences sometimes increases drivers' appetite for risk, as demonstrated when Romain Grosjean and Max Verstappen tangled here in 2015.

Caracciola sat out most of the 1933 racing season after he crashed at Tabac during practice, but the circumstances and severity of his crash were unusual as it was caused by brake failure. Other accidents here, such as Hans Herrmann's in 1955, were of a smaller magnitude, even when it was a more open and inviting corner. Martin Brundle provided an exception to this rule in 1984 when he destroyed his car during practice and was concussed.

It is the chicane and the swimming pool that have been the main focus of attention in ongoing safety work. The chicane in its various locations has been an accident black spot since the Monaco Grand Prix began. It's here that Alberto Ascari and later Paul Hawkins went off into the harbor, and where Lorenzo Bandini suffered fatal burns in 1967. Bandini's accident was exacerbated by the practice of lining the track with straw bales to absorb

leaking fuel caught fire, and the flames spread to the straw bales—fanned by the lurking presence of a TV helicopter hovering lecherously overhead. The race carried on in spite of Bandini's screams of pain.

Armco barriers and a new chicane layout were thought to have reduced the risk to an acceptable level after this, but in 1994, Karl Wendlinger suffered severe head injuries when he spun and broadsided the end of a barrier. Coming shortly after Ayrton Senna's death at Imola, this reminder that safety can never be left to chance was a sharp one.

The architecture of the swimming pool section also left much to be desired, because the presence of brick walls made the entry blind. In 1991, the Italian driver Alex Caffi was lucky to escape with his life when he hit the barrier hard enough to tear his car asunder. Four years later, the Japanese driver Taki Inoue was being towed back to the pits by a truck when the safety car, unsighted, drove into him. Another extension to the harborside enabled the barriers to be moved back, and while this section remains thrillingly quick, the physical consequences of any mistake are relatively minor. But as Verstappen proved when he tapped the inside barrier here and went off during practice for the 2018 race, damaging his car beyond repair before qualifying, "minor" is a relative term.

CHAPTER NINE

MONACO AFTER DARK

THE SOCIAL SCENE

For some, the desire to see and be seen far outweighs any desire to watch race cars. The Monaco Grand Prix sucks in celeb spotters, hangers-on, and wannabe movers and shakers—if fame is your bag, the glitz is irresistible. You never know who you might run into; in 2002, this author was returning to Nice airport via helicopter, expense accounts being more accommodating then, and landed immediately behind one carrying Liza Minelli and her then husband, David Gest.

For many years, there's been no Formula 1 track activity on the Friday of the weekend, ostensibly to observe a public holiday, though the more cynical might conclude that this is a cunning ruse to squeeze visitors' wallets for an extra night's stay and associated expenses. For many people working in and around F1, then, Thursday night is party night, beginning on Red Bull's floating motor home and possibly ending there as well, provided the free booze and nibbles don't run out.

The best F1 party—or worst, depending on your point of view—was Force India team owner Vijay Mallya's cast-of-thousands bash aboard the *Indian Empress*, more an ocean liner than yacht. Unfortunately, Mallya

"THERE ARE MORE FERRARIS PER SQUARE METER THAN ANYWHERE ELSE IN THE WORLD, MORE MONEY PER MILE THAN YOUR LOCAL BANK, AND MORE SUPERMODELS PER SKINNY PROSECCO BOTTLE THAN THE MET GALA."
—*GQ* MAGAZINE

has been unable to leave the UK since 2016, owing to a dispute with the Indian government, who revoked his passport.

Elsewhere, every night is party night. Soon after the engines are shut down, the track opens up and people flood onto the streets, shuffling and gawking and bumping into one another like the first moments of

the zombie apocalypse. Then the music from La Rascasse gets up—maybe they'll even have a DJ performing a live set on the street outside. Gamblers throw their hands in the air to the incessant boom-boom-boom. There's spilled liquid and plastic container detritus everywhere. Mental note: cars will be racing on this very surface, maybe in a handful of hours.

The upscale hotels and casinos are popping. Outside, pinguid British chancers in Thomas Pink shirts—bankers and financial types outside their usual environment, flushed, blotchy and lobster-pink after too long in the sun—line up in Porsche Cayennes and try to scam their way past maitre d's who have all seen their type before. Sorry sir, you can't park there. No, you can't come in. Old social divisions between respectable old and brash new money remain wired in.

Out in the harbor, party hosts compete to offer the best experience and the most exclusive clientele on floating pleasure palaces. Some of these are invitation-only corporate junkets; others merely the super-rich partying among themselves. To rent a superyacht can cost around $100,000 a night, and that's before you get into the champagne and caviar and whatever trinkets are going in the gift bags. Just remember that you'll be expected to take your shoes off before climbing aboard a superyacht. Don't wear "funny" socks.

CHAPTER TEN

IN THE PRESENCE
OF GOD

AYRTON SENNA'S 1988 QUALIFYING LAP

You can find onboard footage of Ayrton Senna's remarkable qualifying lap for the 1989 Monaco Grand Prix—where he went 1.148 seconds faster than his McLaren teammate Alain Prost—on the internet. What you can't find, because it doesn't exist beyond a recreation commissioned by McLaren in 2018, is his magical lap from 1988. There he was 1.427 seconds faster than Prost after a lap that shook even the famously intense Brazilian to his core.

Senna believed that he had been in the presence of some sort of divinity,

that he had achieved some sort of transcendent state, and it scared him.

"I was already just on pole position," he said in an interview with racing journalist Gerald Donaldson. "Then I was fastest by half a second, then by one second, and I was going and I was going and I was going . . . Suddenly, I was about two seconds faster than anybody else, including my teammate with the same car.

"I was kind of driving it by instinct, only I was in a different dimension. It was like I was in a tunnel. I was way over the limit but still able to find even more. Then, suddenly, something just kicked me. I kind of woke up and I realized that I was in a different atmosphere than you normally are. Immediately my reaction was to back off, slow down. I drove back slowly to the pits and I didn't want to go out any more that day.

"It frightened me because I realized I was well beyond my conscious understanding . . . Some moments when I am actually driving just detach me completely from anything else.

"On that day I said to myself, 'That was the maximum for me; no room for anything more.' I never really reached that feeling again."

> "TO RIDE ON A THOUSAND SCREAMING HORSES MAY SEEM AN UNLIKELY SOURCE OF INNER PEACE, BUT LIFE AT 200 MPH CAN LEAD TO SURREAL EFFECTS."
>
> —CLYDE BROLIN

CHAPTER ELEVEN

RACERS WHO RIDE

JOINING MONACO'S TOP SECRET "CHAIN GANG"

The rendezvous was almost surreptitious: over coffee outside the famous Tabac itself, enclosed in the scaffolding that supports the huge grandstand overlooking the corner and the harbor beyond. Me and Alex Wurz, former F1 driver, twice a winner of the Le Mans 24 Hours sports car race, chairman of and spokesman for the Grand Prix Drivers' Association—and ringleader of the secretive F1 "chain gang."

For many months, *F1 Racing* magazine had been angling to join Wurz's clan for one of their bicycle rides to the Italian border and back again. Possible dates came and went, vanishing into the mist. We could track times and places after the fact on Strava, "the social network for athletes," but could we get a firm invitation? No.

Suddenly, we got a date: the Tuesday before the Monaco Grand Prix—a special ride in honor of Sean Edwards, a pro sports car racer and fallen member of the clan, who lost his life in an accident while coaching an amateur driver in Australia. His mother had set up a charitable foundation in his name to campaign for better circuit safety, and the cycling gang was going public to give it a publicity boost.

So, having met up with Wurz and borrowing one of his harem of Scott carbon fiber bikes ("Watch out for the brakes," he cautioned. "They grab a bit."), I found myself outside the Automobile Club de Monaco's offices with a host of professional competitors on four wheels and two: Paul di Resta, Jenson Button, Daniel Ricciardo, David Coulthard, Lucas di Grassi were among the active front-line car racers; with a slight sinking of the heart, I recognized pro cyclists Lizzie Armitstead and Tiffany Cromwell. This ride was going to be *fast*. Nico Rosberg waved us off, with a pitying smile in my direction.

It was still early, but the sun was burning off the morning clouds as we set off eastward, turning sharp right at Sainte Dévote down John F. Kennedy Avenue and on to join the grand prix circuit, albeit traveling in the wrong direction, along the quayside and then through the tunnel. Past the Grimaldi Forum and the Japanese Garden, learning the hard way that, yes, the brakes do grab, as a truck cut across the roundabout ahead by the Monte-Carlo Bay Casino.

With the town behind us, the sound of traffic receded as we hugged the coastline to Roquebrun. Fresh air and the hum of thin bicycle tires on asphalt; Monaco might be a stifling goldfish bowl to some, but this is one hell of a coping mechanism. As we passed through Menton, the Col de la Madone, Lance Armstrong's favored training peak at 925 meters above sea level, reared up to the left. One for another day, perhaps.

At Ventimiglia on the Italian border, we turned left and cut inland. I became aware that Ricciardo had bailed out and turned back on the advice of his trainer. We were going too fast and too hard, baby.

The location of the coffee stop is supposedly a secret, but a little digging on the internet should take you there. You'll know it when you walk through the door and find a sticker with cartoon caricatures of Wurz and Button on the window. The coffee, assuredly, was marvelous—short on quantity, high on the jolt factor. Time elapsed? Barely an hour and a half, and yet we'd traveled through three countries, basking in glorious sunshine tempered by a cool Mediterranean breeze. If you think high-rise living and traffic-choked streets are the unavoidable price of preserving wealth, think again.

CHAPTER TWELVE

ALL THE PRETTY PEOPLE

THE CAP FERRAT SET

Progress has made Monaco a busy, thrusting, and congested place. A pleasantly relaxed twenty-minute drive west of Monaco on the winding coastal road, the forested peninsula of Saint-Jean-Cap-Ferrat offers a window onto the bygone Belle Epoque glamour of the French Riviera's past—albeit a window upon which the shutters are gradually being closed as new money sweeps over it.

There is, in effect, one road in and out, traversing the thumb-shaped promontory's rocky spine. It passes the Villa Ephrussi de Rothschild, an elegant villa and garden constructed over the course of seven years in the early twentieth century, and then disperses into a tangle of side roads that bedevil the kind of leviathan SUVs in which today's newly minted wealthy prefer to be conveyed. Explore beyond the sprawl of modern apartment blocks in the center, and beyond the trees you'll still glimpse fragments of Cap Ferrat's louche past.

Noel Coward's song "I Went to a Marvelous Party" parodied the antics in Villa Mauresque, a house originally built by Leopold II of Belgium, the "builder king" whose immense wealth sprang from ivory looted from the Congo. The British author Somerset Maugham acquired it in 1927, and it became a hub for the literary and celebrity set: T. S. Eliot, Rudyard Kipling, Lord Beaverbrook, the Duke and Duchess of Windsor, and Winston Churchill all passed through and enjoyed lavish hospitality. Maugham described Cap Ferrat as "the escape hatch from Monaco for those burdened with taste."

Arrive on the Tuesday of Monaco Grand Prix week and you'll find most of the restaurants clustered around the harborside in the pretty port of Saint Jean Cap Ferrat closed, or unwilling to welcome customers past 9:00 p.m. Once a secluded spot for the wealthy, this is now a burgeoning building site for investment properties that go unoccupied for much of the year. This author stays in one of the many apartments available on Airbnb for a fraction of the price of a Monaco hotel room.

From here you can explore Cap Ferrat on foot and touch its past and future. Slip on your running shoes and jog south towards the rocky headland. There's a traffic jam caused by a truck delivering building supplies to one of the massive apartment complexes

currently under construction. The road is barely wide enough to sustain a footpath.

Jog on past the building site itself. It's going to be *big*. Until the United Kingdom voted to leave the European Union, London's property market was the hottest ticket on the continent. Now it's in freefall as thousands of speculatively constructed luxury high-rise apartments go unsold, and foreign investors look elsewhere. Here's where they're looking, and concrete is still being poured. To live on Cap Ferrat in this decade is to have one's ears permanently assailed by the sound of building works. It was not like this until very recently; Cap Ferrat was where one could party with a degree of discretion. It's no surprise that Prince Rainier chose to live here with his mistress for six years rather than in Monaco.

To the headland and the narrow, uneven path built from rocks and concrete filler; winter storms have flushed away either or both in places, so your eyes flick constantly between the cliff face and the surface underfoot. The westward path past the Crique de la Causinière is blocked by further building works so we stop, cast our eyes upward to the villas of the super-rich—mostly concealed from prying eyes behind high walls—and turn back east, dodging the construction traffic again and working through still narrower roads. Footpaths become a rarity as we pass the Plage des Fossés, so we get off the winding road as soon as we can, turning right onto the dedicated path at the Promenade des Fossettes, passing below rows of umbrella pines and jasmine. Here the only traffic you'll find consists of elegantly dressed elderly ladies walking handbag-sized dogs that bear a curious resemblance to Dame Maggie Smith in her role as the dowager duchess in the television show *Downton Abbey*. To the right, tankers and cruise ships slip by on the rim of the horizon as the sun glitters off the beautiful blue sea.

Rounding the headland and working our way back to the port, minding the uneven surface underfoot, we skirt Paloma Beach, where Graham Hill and his wife spent the morning after his momentous 1965 Monaco Grand Prix victory. The path runs through the restaurant where waiters clad in crisp white T-shirts and shorts dispense coffee to the early risers.

Leap up the steps and ahead you can see the port and the mainland beyond, rearing up sharply to the village of Eze. At the bottom of the cliff, in Villefranche, lies Villa Nellcôte, a vast Belle Epoque mansion that served as the Gestapo headquarters during Germany's occupation of France in World War II, if you believe popular myths. These spring from the swastika motifs discovered in the basement

when the Rolling Stones recorded *Exile on Main Street* here in 1972, a famously debauched episode of sex 'n' drugs and rock 'n' roll.

Our run won't take us that far, though. Passing the port—the fishermen have already left for the day—we zigzag past the construction site for what will be a new yacht club for the super-wealthy and angle gently uphill towards another outcrop, where an elegant pink villa perches above the waterside. This is La Fleur du Cap, originally known as Villa Socoglio. Now owned by the Croatian artist Ana Tzarev, it was once the home of Charlie Chaplin and, later, the legendary womanizer David Niven, whose parties here became the stuff of legend. Reality intersected with fiction throughout Niven's life, for he epitomized the Hollywood notion of the charming British cad, and he was typically cast as rogues and adventurers. It's said that the biggest wreath at his funeral came from the luggage porters of London's Heathrow airport: "To the finest gentleman who ever walked through these halls. He made a porter feel like a king."

Fittingly, the square outside the mansion's doors, where our brisk 5-kilometer run ends, is now known as the Place David Niven, a fact announced by a modest little plaque. All around it, life goes on.

A SUNNY PLACE FOR SHADY PEOPLE: THE RIVIERA IN LITERATURE

It's in Somerset Maugham's book *The Razor's Edge* that the British author committed to print a phrase that bobs back up to the surface when journalists reach for a pithy *bon mot* to sum up the French Riviera's many contrasts: "a sunny place for shady people." Maugham took up residence on Saint-Jean-Cap-Ferrat in the 1920s, drawn by the richness of the local source material—a kaleidoscope of decadent parties, sunny days on the beach, corruption, secrets, and tragedy.

This section of coastline, from Saint-Tropez to the Italian border, had long been a draw for artists and storytellers. Robert Louis Stevenson, author of *Treasure Island*, passed through the area on a tour of Europe with his parents at the age of twelve, and had an extended stay in Monaco and Menton with a friend eleven years later. Alexandre Dumas set part of his 1844 novel *The Count of Monte Cristo* here, and the titular sailor spends six years in a prison off the coast of Marseille. But it was in the twentieth century that more international authors shifted their attentions here, perhaps inspired by Maugham; during the interwar period, his villa was a veritable ants' nest of literary figures, celebrities, and royalty.

Of the great American writers of that era, Ernest Hemingway and F. Scott Fitzgerald are perhaps better known for their residences in Paris, but both gravitated southwards. Fitzgerald's semi-autobiographical *Tender Is the Night*, nevertheless captures the jazz-age decadence of its Antibes setting as it chronicles a doomed alcohol-fueled love triangle. Fitzgerald and his wife, Zelda, moved to Antibes in 1924, and part of the ten-year delay in completing the novel can be accounted for by the number of artistic figures—Hemingway, Dorothy Parker, Pablo Picasso, to name but a few—who enjoyed their hospitality. Hemingway never finished the novel he set in the Riviera milieu, *The Garden of Eden*, though it was published posthumously in 1986.

Graham Greene, author of *Our Man in Havana*, *The Quiet American*, and the Monaco-set *Loser Takes All*, lived in Antibes from 1966 until shortly before his death in 1991. Greene was a complicated and well-connected individual who had also worked for the British intelligence agency MI6 as a spy, under the supervision of Kim Philby, who would later earn notoriety by defecting to Russia. It was partially to avoid scrutiny into his

payments from MI6—that Greene fled to France when his tax advisor was exposed as a crook. Greene lost everything and had to start again, living in a one-bedroom flat in Antibes, rekindling a romance with a married woman, Yvonne Cloetta—with whom he took lunch every day, though she never left her husband—and writing several more novels, including *Travels with My Aunt* and *The Human Factor*.

Curiously, there are very few novels set in Monaco itself, or around the Grand Prix, that carry any great literary merit. *To Catch a Thief*, the book that ultimately sent Grace Kelly to Monaco, was David Dodge's most commercially successful work, but he was a respectable ex-Navy-man who earned his coin principally through travel writing. Greene's novella *Loser Takes All*, published in 1955, is not considered to be among his best, and while Eric Robert Morse's *Monaco* stretches a thin plot across six hundred pages, it was published half a century after the era in which it is set and is so vague on certain details that the reader inevitably wonders at the depth of research. Perhaps to compose fiction that best encapsulates fractured lives within an era of decadence, you need to have been thoroughly embedded in that world, rubbing shoulders with those exiles escaping an unsuitable marriage or a scandalous past . . .

THE MAKING OF *GRAND PRIX*

Periodically, an image of a race car plummeting over the balustrade in Monaco's harbor will circulate on social media; often the people posting it will make the well-intentioned claim that it is Paul Hawkins plunging into the drink during the 1965 Monaco Grand Prix. Look closer and you'll see that while it *is* a Lotus, the make Hawkins was driving, it's actually a Lotus Formula Junior with replica Formula 1 bodywork. The shot is a publicity still for the John Frankenheimer movie *Grand Prix*, and the stunt itself was suggested by Ferrari driver Lorenzo Bandini, who would perish after an accident at that very spot in 1967.

Marrying a soapily melodramatic plot with real-life racing action, *Grand Prix* is above all a supreme technical accomplishment. Making his first film in color, Frankenheimer broke new ground by putting the camera at the heart of the action rather than taking the safe and easy option of back projection, under-cranking, and other fakery. State-of-the-art Cinerama cameras were rigged to a fleet of replica cars—legend has it that Frankenheimer wanted to enter his own team into the championship that year, but even a Hollywood budget couldn't sustain that—and

the crew shot in and around all the events on the 1966 calendar, except for Reims (Clermont-Ferrand doubled for the French GP) and the Nürburgring (which was allied to a rival movie project).

Frankenheimer sent his principal cast—James Garner, Brian Bedford, Yves Montand, and Antonio Sabàto—to be coached in racing techniques, with varying degrees of success. Bedford didn't even have a driving license and had to be replaced by a stunt double, Garner was determined to do his own stunts, and Sabato approached his task with a verve that surpassed his skill. Professional drivers past and present also featured, including retired aces such as Giuseppe Farina. Jochen Rindt, Bruce McLaren, Graham Hill, and Richie Ginther even got dialogue.

The movie begins, like the 1966 season of which it presents an alternative telling, in Monaco, where the presence of Hollywood operatives—many of whom were taken to be somewhat high on their own self-importance—immediately jangled real-life nerves. Perhaps this venue, with its cramped working conditions, wasn't the best place to introduce the F1 grid to their

INERAMA®
DRAMA OF SPEED AND SP

new working companions; the noisy entourage of make-up artists, costumiers, assistant directors, and special effects folk were even documented in the specialist media at the time.

Henry Manney's Monaco Grand Prix report in *Road & Track* was among the most scathing: "The producer had also imported an unlikely collection of clapped-out Formula Juniors with phony exhausts springing out of the boot-lid in true comic-book style. And various pilots, both unemployed and otherwise, had been engaged to motor these around in the 30-miles-per-hour queue beloved of Hollywood directors, sawing furiously at the wheel like Greek taxi drivers."

If there were reservations about the presence of car-mounted cameras—Graham Hill had crashed in a previous race when one fell off the Porsche of Belgian privateer Carel Godin de Beaufort, and the incident still rankled—Hollywood's purse smoothed the way and the two camps rubbed along together. The machinations of the film's plot hinged around a spectacular crash in Monaco, which drove a wedge between the teammates played by Garner and Bedford. Garner's character ended up taking a swim, and Bedford's had a long stay in the hospital.

Although Garner had to take to the water for shots of the aftermath—a task he didn't enjoy, as the harbor is slick with oily residue from boat engines and other who-knows-what—the crash was filmed separately with a dummy at the wheel. To engineer the plunge into the harbor, special-effects man Milt Rice built a hydrogen-powered cannon that in effect fired the car over the edge.

Making the movie fired a life-long passion for motor racing in Garner. When the film was released, the critical notices weren't entirely kind, owing largely to the hokey plot, but nobody could dispute the power and impact of the action sequences. None of them even vaguely resembled the machinations of taxi drivers, Greek or otherwise. It's now a revered piece of celluloid art for motor racing fans, who haven't been well served in this arena; you would take *Grand Prix* over *Days of Thunder* or *Driven* any day. Only Steve McQueen's largely plotless *Le Mans*, and *Rush*, the 2013 recreation of the James Hunt/Niki Lauda rivalry, have come close to putting the visceral thrill of racing on screen at a level of accuracy that passes muster.

As Garner himself said, "At the end of three hours, you felt as though you'd been in the races, not at the races."

THE TALE OF THE MISSING DIAMOND

The Jaguar Formula 1 team led a brief but turbulent existence, during which they consistently failed to deliver on any promise whatsoever. Their only real success was in generating headlines, none shriller than when they attached $300,000 diamonds to the noses of their cars for the 2004 Monaco Grand Prix . . . and then lost one of them.

Or did they?

Jaguar always wrangled attention brilliantly. Every year in Monaco, even if the cars weren't at the front of the grid—or anywhere near it—the team would be the winner when it came to celebrities in the garage. Monaco 2004 represented the pinnacle of Jaguar's achievements as the team announced a tie-in with the forthcoming all-star heist movie sequel *Ocean's Twelve*, starring the likes of George Clooney, Matt Damon, and Brad Pitt—also in attendance at the Grand Prix, naturally. With such megastardom in the house, the two diamonds, on loan from Steinmetz, were almost surplus to requirements, but perhaps the connection with a movie based on the world's biggest diamond heist was a plot synergy the commercial people could not resist.

Drivers Mark Webber and Christian Klien qualified twelfth and fourteenth—tabloid journalists rubbed their hands at the prospect of describing the performance as "lacking sparkle"—and Klien, then aged twenty-one and racing in his first Monaco Grand Prix, contrived to crash at the hairpin on the opening lap. The car wasn't recovered until the end of the race, whereupon the diamond was found to be absent.

If it had ever been there, of course. Most F1 insiders doubted that a serious competitor would knowingly impede their aerodynamics, or suffer the additional weight of the diamonds' mountings, even around Monaco. Nav Sidhu, then Jaguar's head of communications, now the co-owner of a successful boutique agency in London's Fitzrovia, still won't be drawn on whether the business of the missing diamond was simply a stunt. Certainly, though, PR-wise it was the biggest heist Jaguar ever pulled off.

LAS VEGAS-ON-THE-SEA

The complex relationship between how people perceive Monaco as it is, how it differs from what they think it should be, and what they believe it used to be is best expressed by the society columnist Taki's screed in which he lamented the passing of a certain glamour and gentility from the principality, replaced by an invasive nouveau riche vulgarity expressed in steel and glass and concrete.

Describing the summer of 1960, in which he entertained the actress Janet Leigh, then married to Tony Curtis, and her friend Jean Martin—wife of Rat Pack hub Dean Martin—in the south of France, he wrote, "We had a very good time boating around the various beaches during the day, dancing in Monte Carlo in the evening, Monaco being not only Russian- and vulgarian-free back then, but also looking like Ruritania-sur-mer rather than Las Vegas-on-the-sea."

Taki—real name Panagiotis Theodoracopulos—is a self-styled provocateur and, though he has a fondness for describing himself as "a poor little Greek boy," is the son of a shipping magnate and has never been compelled to work for a living. It has ever been the case that the entrenched plutocracy looks down upon newly minted wealth.

Over the past two decades, many op-eds have slavishly adhered to Taki's template, suggesting that Monaco has lost its élan in the course of its rush to build modern high-rise apartments to accommodate such despised arrivistes. The question we must ask: Is the genteel Monaco of *temps perdu* a fictive construct, projected through a rose-tinted lens?

A 1977 *Rolling Stone* article by Donald Katz, titled "The Prince and the Paupers," pointedly channeled the spirit of Hunter S. Thompson's *Fear and Loathing in Las Vegas* by using the author's supposed mission to interview Princess Caroline as a conceit to take a prurient peek at what was lurking under the rocks: "I was going to Monaco to see the fruits of a great labor, which had revived the legendary fairy-tale image of the place and blown it out of all proportion. The efforts of Harvard Business School graduates, Las Vegas pit bosses, Aristotle Onassis, a few American ex-diplomats— and an Oscar-winning actress from Philadelphia—have seemingly created a profitable Xanadu out of a little rock in the French Riviera that was once the haven of the very rich."

During the course of the story, Katz toured through a host of twentieth-century Monaco tropes: dead-eyed gamblers rich and poor, from dapper gentlemen nonchalantly flipping high-stakes tokens onto the baize in the old casino to the shuffling denizens of the American-style casinos down the hill. The overall picture was one of established wealth and class sitting in uneasy coexistence with brash new arrivals, despising their existence while quietly pocketing their money.

Rewind in stages through Monaco's history. It's been like this since Charles III re-engineered the principality's moribund fortunes by setting the casino economy in motion. And why not? For the Grimaldi family, the past eight centuries have been a tale of survival, often against the odds. It's quite natural that this dynasty came to embrace its present role. Without a reason to come here—whether that reason is to watch the Grand Prix, play the odds in the casinos, or to obey the tenet that once one has acquired money, the prudent next step is not to give it away again—Monaco would have remained an obscure patch of real estate at the bottom of a cliff.

Like any successful casino, Monaco is a carefully engineered business in which the house always wins.

PAGE 55

William Grover-Williams won the 1929 French Grand Prix from the back of the grid (which was, as per custom at the time, decided by a lottery system).

PAGE 66

Rudolf Caracciola (right, in white) and Mercedes colleagues acknowledge the victorious Luigi Fagioli with a Nazi salute after the 1935 Monaco Grand Prix.

PAGE 69

Ferdinand Porsche (second from right) had a hand in Grand Prix racing regulations during the 1930s, and was the architect of several cars that pushed those rules to the limits.

PAGE 87

Small-scale manufacturers such as Gordini (pictured here at Reims in 1952) played a vital role in reestablishing top-level motor racing after World War II.

PAGE 95

The great Juan Manuel Fangio claimed his last Formula 1 at Monaco in 1957, driving a Maserati. He lost the lead on the opening lap to Stirling Moss (Vanwall) and Peter Collins (Ferrari), but they crashed at the chicane, as did Mike Hawthorn (Ferrari), and the wreck sat there for the rest of the race.

232

PAGE 128

During the 1960s, the Formula 1 grid was usually limited to twenty-three entries, of which the fastest sixteen were allowed to start, but organizers often permitted bigger grids for the support series—with predictably chaotic results. Here in the 1962 Formula Junior race, Swedish driver Ulf Norinder launches his Lotus 22 over the back of Curt Bardi-Barry's Cooper T59.

PAGE 140-141

Jochen Rindt missed the 1969 Monaco Grand Prix while he recovered from injuries sustained when his Lotus 49's rear wing failed at the Spanish Grand Prix.

PAGE 178-179

French President Charles de Gaulle made his only official visit to Monaco in 1960. Relations would take a turn for the worse over the following two years.

PAGE 189

Australian driver Paul Hawkins crashed into the harbor on lap seventy-nine of the 1965 Monaco Grand Prix. After his Lotus was recovered, his mechanics attached a lifebuoy to the car with the words "swimming kangaroo" daubed on it.

PAGE 222

French singer Francoise Hardy played the role of Lisa in the movie *Grand Prix*. She had previously represented Monaco in the Eurovision Song Contest, a famously kitsch annual musical competition.

INDEX

236

237

PHOTO CREDITS